The Fifty Judo Principles

Charles Mack

ISBN-13: 978-1544045887

1 FIRST PRINCIPLE

Join a good club.

To develop judo technique so that one can use it with skill and power, it is absolutely essential, especially for the beginner, to receive good instruction from an experienced instructor who is a Black Belt, preferably 2nd Dan and above. Instruction by itself however is not sufficient. It is also necessary to have opportunities to put that which one is taught into practice. In other words, one must regularly practise with other judo enthusiasts in a competitive manner, each of you attempting to get the better of the other via the use of judo techniques. And in order to practise judo techniques in an all-out manner but without injuring each other, you practise on mats. The most popular type of judo mat is the Japanese straw mat with a vinyl cover. This measures only six feet by three feet but when a number of them are put down side by side and fixed in position an area large enough for judo training is obtained.

Now, in order to have all of these three things (instruction, competition, facilities), you must become a member of a Judo Club. Not any club mark you but a good, reputable club where they have teachers who are both experienced in practising judo themselves and also in teaching it. An experienced judo player with no teaching experience is not the ideal teacher. Nor is the teacher who has not much personal experience himself of actually doing competitive judo even though he may have teaching experience. There is no doubt that the best teachers of judo are those men who have had a great deal of personal experience as competitive judo players whose experience and skill are indicated by their judo grade and who then go on to acquire teaching experience. In Japan, where the greatest judo artists in the world are produced, instructors rarely hold less than 5th Dan grade. However, it is not necessary to expect to be taught by a 5th Dan instructor in clubs outside of Japan as this grade outside of that country is held by very few men. And one more thing regarding what may be termed the ideal judo teacher is that although there are many fine judo men who have never trained in Japan, it certainly seems that the Japan-trained judo man (Japanese and non-Japanese) does make the best teacher. This is because he has consciously and otherwise acquired a great deal of knowledge from being exposed for such a long time to the situation in Japan, where the number of people practising judo is so large, where the technique and knowledge is so advanced, where the variations of the same technique and the subtlety of their application are greater than anywhere else in the world, and where everything concerning judo is on such a grand scale. And although of course it is not possible for a judo player to practise everything he observes while he is training in Japan, the knowledge he acquires from observation, instruction, and intelligent reflection during his stay there can be used to great advantage for his pupils when he teaches judo.

The ideal club therefore is one where the instruction is first class, where there are a large number of keen judo enthusiasts to practise with, and where the facilities are good. This sort of club does exist in places like London where you have such famous clubs as the Budokwai, the Renshuden, the Judokan, the London Judo Society, the Croydon Judo Club, etc. However, in the provinces, you will most likely have to be content with training at much smaller clubs. These, however, if the instruction is good and a tradition of hard training exists, can and do produce strong and skilful judo men. The author himself started at such a club, The Newcastle Judo Club of Newcastle Upon Tyne, where there were plenty of keen judo men to practise with and where he had the good fortune of being instructed by the club's leading instructors, Mr. George Bamford, and Mr. Leslie Crowe.

One final word. Join a good club, but do not think that because you do this your progress will be automatic, because it will not. Only hard training on your part can enable you to progress satisfactorily.

2 SECOND PRINCIPLE

From the beginning, stick to one side, i.e. do either right-handed or left-handed techniques: do not do both.

For those genuinely ambitious people who have a strong desire to get a high grade in judo, or to win championships, or to develop tremendously powerful judo technique, the only way to achieve these ambitions is to develop your judo repertoire on one side only, on the right or on the left. If you are a natural right-hander, which the vast majority of people are, you practise what are called right-handed techniques, and if you are a natural left-hander, you practise left-handed techniques.

There are, I am well aware, in Japan and elsewhere, good judo players who are not of this opinion and who themselves do left and right-handed techniques. And what is more they do have a lot of success in doing so. However, one cannot deny the facts when one gets down to brass tacks with this controversy. And the facts are that the men who win the big championships in Japan and elsewhere are, with very, very few exceptions, judo players who specialize in techniques on one side only.

And when one studies the judo players who have had success even though they practised right and left-handed techniques, we find that they were exceptionally talented individuals with a great capacity for hard training. Therefore if you wish to achieve your potential in judo, do not be deceived into thinking that practising right and left technique will enable you to do it, but stick to one side.

The temptation to ignore this principle is at times quite great. And this is especially so when you find that your opponent does not seem to be affected at all with the techniques which you are attempting from one side only. Or when you are finding difficulty in preventing your opponent from countering you when you come in for a throw, and so on. Strange as it may seem, it is just those terribly frustrating circumstances which provide you with the best opportunities for developing your skill and power. Because if you stick to your guns as it were and do not allow yourself to be disheartened by your inability to get the better of your opponent, you will find that you are forced to attack with greater determination, speed, timing, and a more scientific application of your technique. In other words what is happening is that your whole mind and body are being alerted by the competition which your opponent is offering you by his determination not to allow you to throw him, by his countering you, etc. And frustrating as it may be at times, the fact of the matter is that without it the development of

3

real expertise and power would not be possible. And once you realise the vast importance of this competition as the main element in your development as a judo expert, you will if you are wise seek out and not avoid the opponents who can best provide you with it.

One very convincing argument in favour of specializing in one-sided technique is the following. In judo, one's ability to resist throwing attempts by one's opponent gets gradually stronger and stronger. This comes about by being constantly attacked by the various judo throwing techniques and the more one is attacked with these the stronger one's ability to resist them becomes. It is quite a natural process and comes to all judoists in time. Now then, in a large competitive judo society such as exists in Japan, you have a good opportunity to develop a very good defence against both right-handed and left-handed throwing techniques, because although most Japanese judoists are right-handers, there are also a large number of left-handers. Some of the latter are not natural left-handers but have decided to specialize in left-handed technique because of the strategic advantages which being a left-hander offers. Now the argument is that if you have these opportunities to build up a defence both against men who specialize in nothing but right-handed techniques and against men who specialize in nothing but left-handed techniques, what chance does a man who attempts to do both right and left techniques have of throwing you? It stands to reason that if you can resist the throwing attempts of left handers and also the attempts of right handers, who due to their concentrating on one side only both become extremely powerful on their respective sides, then the man who halves his chances of developing great power because he does both right and left techniques will have very little chance of throwing you. Of course, one man who has greater experience than another will be able to throw the latter with either right or left techniques. But this proves nothing and is not a refutation of the one-sided principle, due to the fact that one man has an advantage over the other. And the principle of sticking to one side is based on the assumption, as any intelligent principle must be, that no party has any advantage over the other but that both are equal in every respect, especially in respect of experience, weight, and strength.

Finally, if ever you do decide to add to your repertoire a technique on the side which you do not specialize in, give a great deal of time and thought to your choice of technique. You should also seek the advice of a high-grade judo man with a lot of practical experience behind him, Failing to take these precautions will probably result in your practising a technique which will not combine well with the rest of your techniques. And as the main reason for building up a technique on the other side is to enable you to use it for the purpose of feints, strategisms, etc., you can imagine how foolish it would be to develop a technique which would not enable you to do this naturally by its not combining well with the rest of your repertoire.

3 THIRD PRINCIPLE

Do techniques which are suitable for your height.

When deciding which kind of techniques to specialize in so that you can be absolutely sure that you will give yourself every possible chance of achieving your true judo potential, the main thing to be considered is your height. This is so because in the case of some judo techniques, unless you are tall, you will never become very powerful via the practice of such techniques. This is also true in reverse for the short man. In other words, unless you are short, you will never become very good at judo via the practice of certain techniques. And also on the other hand, shortness is a definite handicap when it comes to executing other techniques. So if you are tall, you go in for what are sometimes referred to as the tall man's techniques. And if you are short, you practise what are called sometimes the short man's techniques.

In the case of those people who are very tall or very short, the choice of techniques is quite straight-forward and any competent teacher will be able to put you on the right track. Generally speaking, the tall judo man specializes in Uchi-mata and Osoto-gari. These two techniques are musts for the tall man and if he chooses any other two techniques for his two main guns as it were, he will be extremely foolish. There are other techniques which a tall man can do and probably will do once he has mastered these two techniques but he should not bother with them until he has acquired this mastery. The right-hander of course must do these two techniques on the right, and the left-hander must do them on the left.

The next thing to do is to learn how to combine them well with each other so that when your opponent reacts against an attack with one of them, you can easily take advantage of this reaction and throw him with the other one. The ability to combine techniques in this fashion is absolutely necessary to a judo man if he wants to be able to make the greatest possible use of the techniques in which he specializes. That is why he must use techniques which enable him to do this smoothly and with speed. Uchi-mata and Osoto-gari are two such techniques.

These two techniques, the execution of which requiring as it does a large physical movement, are called Major Techniques. And these are undoubtedly the best ones to practise for the development of judo power and naturalness of movement, both of which are the hallmark of the judo expert. However, the minor techniques are also to be practised once you have gained a good idea of the execution of your favourite major techniques. What are very good minor techniques to practise for the Uchi-mata and Osoto-gari specialist, combining well as they do with these two techniques, are Ouchi-gari, Kosoto-gari or Kosoto-gake, and Tsuri-komi-ashi.

Ouchi-gari is an excellent technique to turn into after you have attempted Uchi-mata but failed to bring it off. What often happens when you try Uchi-mata is that the opponent will react so violently against it that he weakens his balance to his rear, giving you an excellent opportunity to bring off a throw with Ouchi-gari. This particular combination, Uchi-mata and Ouchi-gari, is the favourite combination of Mr. Hasegawa, a famous Japanese judo star.

The next two techniques, Kosoto-gari and Kosoto-gake, are both two of the favourite techniques of Mr. Maeda and Mr. Oda, two tall Japanese judo stars. They are also two of the pet techniques of Mr. Jon Bluming, a very tall Dutch judo expert, whom I knew at the Kodokan in Japan, and who had a lot of success with these techniques against his shorter Japanese opponents. Both of these techniques combine very well with Uchi-mata in the following way. You can throw your opponent quite easily with them after you have merely feinted with Uchi-mata and caused him by this feint to bring his legs closer together or to push his knee inwards in anticipation of your attack. This kind of reaction gives you an excellent chance of bringing off a throw with Kosoto-gari or Kosoto-gake. If he reacts towards his own rear but keeps his leg fairly wide apart, you will of course follow up your Uchi-mata feint with an Ouchi-gari, which is a better technique against a wide-legged stance.

Ouchi-gari is also widely used among Japanese judo players in conjunction with Osoto-gari, and if they fail to throw their opponent with it, they quickly whip their reaping leg out from in between his legs and hurl themselves into Osoto-gari, using the same leg of course. This particular combination usually involves, say when it is done on the right, trying an Ouchi-gari and then when you sense it is not going to work, rapidly putting your right leg back on to the ground, stepping forward and to your left with your left foot, and then hurling your right leg past his right leg at the back to throw him with Osoto-gari. This combination requires for its success an all-out, non-stop flow of movement, because due to the fact that you have to replace your right foot on to the ground after attempting the Ouchi-gari and also move the left foot to the side and forward, which of course all takes time, your opponent has a chance of recovering his balance. The trick is to do the necessary footwork before he has a chance to replace his left foot on the ground after you have lifted it into the air with your Ouchi-gari. If you can in other words get your right leg behind his right leg before he has replaced his left foot on the ground, you have a good chance of throwing him with your Osoto-gari.

The last minor technique in the list I have given is Tsuri-komi-ashi. Now this technique is difficult to do if, like most tall men, you take a high hold with your right hand on your opponent's collar or high up on his lapel. If you are a left-hander, you will do this with your left hand. I shall describe the technique on the right, where you sweep and press your opponent's left front shin with the sole of your right foot and pull him over it with a pulling and lifting action of both hands, particularly your right hand. If you hold high up with your right hand this action is difficult to effect. If however you hold lower down on your opponent's jacket, preferably near his left armpit, the powerful pulling and lifting action necessary in the case of this technique can be easily effected. This technique can be used with great effect after having first feinted with either Osoto-gari or Uchi-mata, but preferably the latter, and especially against a man who stands rather square on to you or to the left. The judo expert who has made Tsuri-komi-ashi famous is Anton Geesink of Holland, who was the first non-Japanese to become world judo champion. He uses it as a solo technique and also makes great use of it after he has made a feint with another technique, usually right Uchi-mata, which has for years put the fear of death into judo players from every country in the world. Geesink, however, takes a low right-hand hold on his opponent's jacket quite near the armpit. And it is this hold undoubtedly which enables him to have such wonderful success with his Tsuri-komi-ashi.

Finally, although the minor techniques which have been mentioned are used a great deal in combinations, etc., with other techniques, they can as we have seen in the case of Geesink and his Tsuri-komi-ashi, be used by themselves as solo techniques, the most popular of which is Ouchi-gari.

For the short judo player who wishes to get the beat out of himself as it were, the best major techniques for him to spend most of his time on are undoubtedly Morote-seoinage and/or Tsuri-komi-goshi. Both of these techniques enable the short man to throw very tall and heavy people, as they enable him to get right underneath his opponents and bring to bear very powerful hand movement and strength on the upper part of their bodies while at the same time destroying their balance from below by a strong backward and upward movement with his back and buttocks. And it is via techniques like these which, in judo anyway, do enable a man who is much shorter and lighter than his opponent to defeat him. However, if he does not select techniques which are good for the small man, in other words those techniques which enable him to get right underneath his large opponents so that he can use his arm, back, and rear hip strength and power to their full, he will always due to his inferior weight and strength be at a serious disadvantage when against a heavier opponent of equal experience as himself. And of course, and even more so some teachers claim, the same care must be exercised by even tall, heavy men when choosing the techniques which they will specialize in. Because it can be seen how difficult it would be for a tall man to get underneath a shorter man with a trick like Morote-seoinage or Tsuri-komi-goshi in order to position his right arm for the upward leverage necessary in both of these techniques. Likewise the short man who foolishly spends his time developing the tall man's techniques, will find that although he will have a lot of success of course against those who are not as tall as himself, when he comes against tall, heavy, powerful and experienced opponents, his lack of height and body stretch will seriously handicap him when attempting these throws.

The minor techniques which are favourites with the short judo player are if he is right-handed, Kouchi-gari, which technique requires his reaping the inside of his opponent's right heel with either the sole or achilles tendon part of his right foot; Deashi-barai and Okuriashi-barai, the execution of which is very similar in both techniques. The former is done by sweeping the opponent's left foot in a diagonal direction with the sole of your right foot. The latter also is done by sweeping the opponent's left foot with your right sole but instead of making a diagonal sweeping action as in Deashi-barai, you make a direct sweeping action across your own body to your left. This is the way a right-hander does these techniques. The left-hander simply reverses everything.

These three techniques are of course techniques in their own right and enable you to throw your opponent via a direct attack with one of them. In other words you can use them without necessarily combining them with other techniques. They are of course also used in combination with each other and with your major techniques. Each can, in other words, be used as a feinting technique with one of the other two or with one of your major techniques. And likewise of course you can use the major techniques as feinting techniques with these three minor techniques. These three techniques if used in intelligent conjunction with your major techniques will also enable you to take advantage of all the various positions in which your opponent finishes up after managing to escape from an attack either with one of these three or with your major technique or techniques.

One of the reasons why Kouchi-gari, Deashi-barai, and Okuriashi-barai are useful for small men to specialize in is because of the speed with which they have to be done if one is to have a chance of throwing one's opponent with them. And of course small men are usually much faster in their movement than big men. Again we see that a small man must constantly be searching for the best way to use whatever advantages his smallness and speed provide him with. Failing to do this can only result in his being beaten every time he meets a much bigger man in contest.

The Japanese judo men if they are short will, to pull off a throw like Morote-seoinage or Tsuri-komi-goshi, often push you backwards to set you up for the forward throwing action of either of these two techniques. The reason why he pushes you backwards first is to trick you into resisting the push and therefore weaken your balance forward. Or he will try to bring about the same thing by first trying Kouchi-gari, which again will, because it is a rear technique, cause you to push your body forward and give him a chance to bring off his forward technique. And of course he will, in order to weaken your resistance to a rear technique like Kouchi-gari, first attempt or simply feint with Morote-seoinage or Tsuri-komi-goshi and then take advantage of this momentary weakness to your rear by throwing you with Kouchi-gari.

Another very popular combination of techniques used by the smaller judo man in Japan is Tsuri-komi-goshi and Deashi-barai or Okuriashi-barai. Very often in resisting the former, you will resist to your left and give him a chance to throw you by sweeping your left foot away from under you with either of the latter. Which one he uses will often be determined by just how you resist the hip throw. And in reverse he will attempt or merely feint with the foot throws which has the effect of taking your mind off the fact that he also has another technique up his sleeve, and then throw you to the front with his Tsuri-komi-goshi. Two of the greatest experts with the combination of Tsuri-komi-goshi and Deashi-barai or Okuriashi-barai are undoubtedly Mr. Osawa, one of the leading judo teachers at the Kodokan in Tokyo, who does both of these techniques on the left as he is a left-hander, and Mr. Shinohara, an old friend of mine, who was the captain of the judo team of Meiji University in Tokyo one of the strongest judo colleges in Japan. Mr. Shinohara, who because he is a right-hander does his combination on the right. He is now teaching judo in the United States, where in judo circles he is very well known thanks to this combination of his having won for him the title of American Judo Champion.

For those of average height, the choice of techniques in which to specialize is not so straightforward as it is for those who are tall or short. The reason why it is simple in the case of tall or short people is due to the fact that in the vast majority of cases the tall man's opponents will be shorter than himself and this will enable him to use the tall man's techniques (Uchi-mata, Osoto-gari, etc.) against them with great effect. In reverse, the short man will, most of the time anyway, have opponents who are taller than he is, and if he has become proficient in what we have seen are the best techniques for the short man to practise, he will also obtain very good results against his opponents. For the person who is neither tall nor short, however, he will often meet those who are taller than himself, those who are shorter than himself, and of course those who are, like himself, in the average height category. As we have already seen how difficult it would be for a short man to throw a tall man with a tall man's technique or for a tall man to throw a short man with a short man's technique, what technique or techniques must the man of average height do in order to have a chance against most of his opponents, who as we have already seen will often be taller or shorter than himself and often the same height as himself? It seems that, if he wants to have a chance against men of such variety in height, he must specialize in one major technique which he will employ against opponents who are shorter than himself, and in another major technique which he will employ against opponents who are taller than himself. And undoubtedly the best techniques which will enable him to do this in the most effective manner are Uchi-mata and Tai-otoshi.

The former will enable him to throw those who are shorter than himself, and the latter will enable him to throw those who are taller than himself. The beauty about specializing in these two techniques is that they enable you to have a good chance against not only tall or short opponents, but either of these techniques can also be used effectively against opponents who are the same height as yourself.

4 FOURTH PRINCIPLE

Place great emphasis on Tachiwaza (Throwing Technique) as opposed to Newaza (Groundwork Technique).

This does not of course mean that Groundwork is not important. It is very important indeed. But it is not nearly as important as Tachiwaza (see Fifth Principle).

Undoubtedly, and this is the main consensus of opinion among high-grade Japanese judo masters, the real test of skill in judo is to have to throw with power an experienced judo man. If this person is also much heavier, physically stronger, and much younger than yourself, then of course to have to throw him is a greater test of skill again. So when a person claims that the throwing techniques of judo are more difficult to master than the groundwork techniques of judo, he means when they have to be done against experienced judo players. Of course it is also very difficult to overpower an experienced opponent with the holding, joint, and strangulation techniques of Groundwork, but from the point of view of pure skill not nearly so difficult as throwing him. This is because in Groundwork it is much easier to take advantage of your strength and weight than it is in the throwing techniques. Strength and weight are an advantage in Tachiwaza too, but it can be seen by even those with limited experience in judo that it is considerably more difficult a task to control an opponent lighter and weaker than oneself by the use of your weight and strength advantage in Tachiwaza than in Newaza.

And it is because of this reason that many physically strong, heavy people tend to spend a lot of the time they devote to their judo training on the practising of those techniques which are usually applied when both men are on the ground.

Another reason why some people find themselves drifting into groundwork, and this is so especially amongst beginners, is because in the practice of groundwork technique it is easier to notice or sense one's own progress in often quite a dramatic fashion, which of course is the source of a great deal of personal satisfaction. But why it is much more common to experience this feeling of personal progress if one does a lot of groundwork is simply because other people are not doing as much of it as oneself, and this naturally enables one to defeat one's opponent quite easily when practising groundwork. So this gives one the impression that one's progress is more rapid than it really is. And this can in turn encourage people to practise even less Tachiwaza than they have been doing, due to the fact that, at first anyway, it is quite difficult when practising throwing techniques to feel that you are making much progress. This is due, first of all, to the inherent difficulty of controlling your opponent so well that you can actually throw him with force on to his back. Secondly, it is because at most judo clubs, most of the members do actually practise throwing techniques much more than they practise groundwork techniques, and consequently become more skilful in the former than in the latter, which of course makes it more difficult to beat them by throwing techniques than by groundwork techniques.

In spite of these difficulties, there is no doubt at all that the people who make the best progress in judo and the ones who eventually win top class contests are those who persevere with their attempts to master the throwing techniques of this art by spending most of their training time on Tachiwaza and the rest of it on groundwork, and not the other way round. The reasons for this are first that in order to be able to defeat an opponent on the ground it is necessary to get him there, and unless one can throw with skill and power, it is very difficult to do this, especially against an opponent who has through experience developed great resistance to all kinds of throwing techniques. And so you find the man who has good groundwork technique unable to use it because of his inability to get his opponent to the ground due to his lack of skill and power in throwing techniques. And scoring a point by throwing this kind of opponent on to his back in contest is of course out of the question for the groundwork specialist who usually does not have the necessary power in his throwing techniques to manage this. On the other hand, the specialist in throwing techniques can score points against any type of opponent by throwing them on to their back, and he does also have a good chance of scoring points in groundwork too due to his ability to get his opponent to the ground with throwing technique. In other words, if his throwing attempt fails to score for him a point, he very often finishes up nevertheless in a position on the ground where he has an advantage over his opponent. And if he has practised a reasonable amount of groundwork, which of course he is expected to, he will be able to secure a point by the application of a groundwork technique.

The other main reason why the man who spends a lot of his time developing the throwing techniques of judo finishes up eventually becoming more effective as a judo contest player than the man who mostly does groundwork and never really develops powerful throwing technique is because via the constant practice of major throwing techniques, he not only develops almost uncanny skill in the execution of throws, but also develops great physical strength and power, a wonderful sense of timing, and very speedy reactions to all sorts of situations. And when at a later stage of his development he turns his attention to groundwork techniques, he finds that all of these attributes stand him in great stead in becoming expert in these techniques as well as those of Tachiwaza.

The object of the really ambitious judo player, therefore, should be to develop an all round expertise in both the throwing techniques and the groundwork techniques of judo. And undoubtedly the best way to go about this is in the early stages of his development to concentrate more on Tachiwaza than on Newaza, and then gradually to develop the techniques of the latter too so that he will have ability and confidence in both aspects of his art. If he attempts to do it in reverse, that is to give most of his time and thought in the early stages of his training to Groundwork rather than to the throwing techniques, it certainly seems, in most cases anyway, that his chances of becoming a judo champion will be greatly reduced.

5 FIFTH PRINCIPLE

From the time that you take up Judo, you should get into the habit of doing plenty of Newaza (Groundwork Technique), but, especially in the early stages of your training, do not treat it as important a part of your training as Tachiwaza (Throwing Technique).

Although, as was pointed out in the Fourth Principle, the best way to develop as a judo player is to concentrate more on Tachiqaza than on Newaza, it must not be assumed by this that you should exclude the practice of Newaza altogether from your training. On the contrary, you should introduce the practice of groundwork technique into your training schedule as soon as you take up the art. If this is not done right from the outset, there is the very great likelihood that the practice of Newaza will never become for you a natural part of your judo repertoire. And this of course would be a great pity from the point of view of developing the confidence necessary to becoming a successful contest judo player. Because there is no doubt at all that without groundwork ability one's confidence does suffer.

By confidence, we mean the faith in one's skill and power to enable one to handle every conceivable situation which may arise when taking part in a judo contest. Now what can be termed a frequently recurring situation is that of attempting against your opponent a throwing technique, which does not actually score for you a point, due to your opponent having twisted himself out of the throw, or having done something else which may prevent your scoring a point against him for a throw. However, even though his efforts may save him from defeat by being thrown on to his back, he will nevertheless still find himself on the ground with you either on your feet or lying on top of him, both of which positions are advantageous to you. These positions are advantageous to you because they offer you excellent opportunities to simply come down on top of him in the first case and secure a hold-down or some other groundwork technique, and in the second case, where you are already lying on top of him, to simply consolidate your already strong position by making the changes in it necessary to applying a groundwork technique. Now, unless you have confidence in your groundwork ability, you will be reluctant to enter into groundwork with your opponent even when it is obvious that you are, as seen in examples just given, at a definite advantage. Because these positions are only advantageous to you if you have groundwork skill. If you do not have this skill, you will find that as soon as you attempt to control him on the ground, even though you may at first have the strong upper position, he will if he has groundwork skill soon turn the tables on you and defeat you with a newaza technique. But if you have ability in groundwork, even though it may be inferior to your opponent's, you can very often defeat him on the ground if first you find yourself in a position of advantage such as the ones just given. And as, as has already been said, these situations crop up again and again, you can see just how many opportunities for defeating your opponent you will miss if you never, by practice, develop the necessary confidence in your Newaza ability to take advantage of them.

In the situations just described, being above your opponent as you are, it is you who takes the initiative usually as to whether groundwork commences or not. In the reverse situation, when your opponent has the upper position of advantage, you are not in such a happy position at all. And it is in this situation particularly, where you have no choice but to fight on the ground, where groundwork confidence is most necessary.

In the former case, where you have the position of advantage, what you need most is offensive or attacking groundwork skill, so that you can follow up your advantage and defeat your opponent with a groundwork technique before he has a chance to neutralize this advantage which you wield over him for a few brief moments. In the latter case, however, where your opponent has an advantage over you, what you need is defensive groundwork skill. This kind of skill, although not nearly as admirable an attribute in a judo man as the positive attacking kind of skill, is nevertheless an essential part of the all-round judo man's repertoire, enabling him as it does to escape from the various groundwork techniques.

There are many other situations which frequently occur in judo contest which offer convincing proof of the absolute necessity to develop groundwork skill, of both the offensive and defensive kind, but the two examples given serve best to exemplify this necessity most.

6 SIXTH PRINCIPLE

Practise frequently and regularly.

All other advice can be said to be quite secondary to that contained in this principle. For without frequent and regular practice, you will never develop the naturalness of movement, speed, timing, determination, etc., which are the prerequisites to the application of any kind of intelligent instruction. It is a fallacy, unfortunately a very common one, to assume that because one has a good instructor and good facilities, that one will therefore make satisfactory progress. Good instruction and good facilities are important to satisfactory progress of course, but unless a student attempts, under reasonably competitive conditions, to apply that which he is taught, by practising frequently and regularly, his rate of progress will be most discouraging indeed.

What then, people often ask, is meant by frequent and regular practice? Should a person train every day? And if so, how many hours per day? One hour? One and a half hours? Or two hours? And how intense should one's training be? Should it be a non-stop kind or should one have plenty of rests in between practice bouts? Is it more beneficial to train hard for one hour every day or to train in a leisurely fashion for two hours every day? Another question which is often asked is whether it is wiser to train hard every day for an hour or to train hard every other day for two hours. Or, is it necessary to think in terms of training every day or even every other day at all? Could one not make progress at a reasonable pace if one did say only a couple of training sessions at one's club per week for about an hour or an hour and a half each time?

Well, of course, the number of times a person trains per week and the length and intensity of each training session will depend on the individual. A young man with very little responsibilities will for example be able to devote more time to practising than will an older man with say professional and marital responsibilities. And a person who is studying for some kind of examination to do with his working career will be foolish to spend too much time on practising if it might interfere with his chances of passing the examination. Whereas someone who has finished with examinations or someone who has no interest in such things can practise as much as their enthusiasm and will power will allow them to.

To be more precise, so as to give you some idea as to what kind of training is applicable in your own individual case, let us start with the man who has enough enthusiasm to aspire to becoming a high-grade judo player.

In his case, he will have to train from four to six times per week, depending on the kind of competition he can expect to meet up with in contests. This competition will vary from country to country. In Japan, for example, the very good players train five to six days per week for two hours per session. In England or other countries outside of Japan, where the competition is not so intense, four training sessions per week is usually enough to enable a man to acquire the skill and power he will need when he eventually starts to compete with the cream of the crop as it were. These sessions should have a duration of one and a half to two hours. And this training should be done regularly. That is, it should be done week in and week out, and preferably on the same days each week. This regularity makes training much easier than the irregular kind of training which tends to place too much strain on the player's will power. It also ensures fast and satisfactory progress.

Let us next take the person who, although perhaps not as ambitious as the person in the example just given, is nevertheless in the keen category and would like to get a decent grade in judo, but who is not particularly interested in winning championships. Here again, his training schedule will be determined by how enthusiastic a judo community he is a member of, as it is this enthusiasm or lack of it which provides either strong competition or weak competition in the grading contests he takes part in. Generally speaking, however, a training schedule consisting of three one and a half hour training sessions per week is enough to enable this kind of individual to achieve his ambition and get a fairly decent grade without spending years of his life doing it. Again, however, let us stress the importance of the element of regularity in the training schedule, especially in the early stages of his training. Training should be done every week and not only when in the mood as it were. And so that he will not have to make a great effort of will every time he goes to train, his training should become for him a very rewarding habit, and this can no doubt best be achieved by training on the same days each week, and not on different days as many people try to do.

It is not to be expected that many people will have enough enthusiasm or time to enable them to practise four times per week, every week, as in the case of those who aspire to winning championships. Nor does it seem that a very large number of people have the necessary will power, even if they have the time and the enthusiasm, to practise the three times per week, every week, as in the case of those who wish to get a fairly high grade without taking too much time about it. We therefore have another category of individuals who although they never become champions or who never speed from one grade to another every time they go into a grading competition, do still make progress at a fairly reasonable pace. These are the ones who practise twice a week, for periods varying from one, one and a half, and two hours. Even twice a week, if done regularly, can enable a person to acquire judo skill and enable him to get a respectably high judo grade.

There are of course those who practise even less than twice a week and who still manage to get fairly proficient. But, if they do this in a fairly short space of time it is usually found that they are individuals who have athletic ability of quite a rare kind and make fast progress especially in the early stages of their judo training. Or, it is found also that the once-a-weeker who is quite skillful has actually been doing judo for much longer than he would care to remember. Because the fact of the matter is that unless a person practises regularly twice a week, it is going to take him a long time to get anywhere, unless, like the individuals already mentioned, he thinks he has more than ordinary aptitude.

It is therefore by far the wisest thing to do if you take up judo to get into the habit straight off of doing two training sessions per week at least. And then when you have acquired skill and a respectable grade, maybe you can reduce this to even less. But if you try to develop skill by practising only once a week or less, you will, generally speaking, take so long in developing the skill that you will get fed up with your lack of progress and give up judo altogether. If you acquire skill via more frequent practice however, you grow to become more enthusiastic about judo and there is very little chance of your giving it up. In Judo, as in everything else, success leads to success. But, also as in everything else, it has to be earned.

7 SEVENTH PRINCIPLE

Develop the habit of thinking about that which your training sessions suggest you should think about.

What is meant by this is that your own practising or training sessions are your greatest possible source of judo knowledge. Instead of wasting your time, therefore, on attempting to solve those problems of a very highly theoretical nature, which judo is replete with, concentrate your intellect on those problems the solution of which will enable you to improve your prowess as a practical judo player. And, undoubtedly, the solution of those problems which constantly beset you when practising with skillful, aggressive opponents at your club will enable you to do this best. If, therefore, after a training session, you allow your mind to dwell on the practices you had during the session, and the particular difficulties and problems which each of your opponents created from the point of view of frustrating your attempts at defeating him, you will give your mind a chance of finding answers to these difficulties and problems. And if you do this regularly, you will, as the Seventh Principle enjoins you, "develop the habit of thinking about that which your training sessions suggest you should think about."

Some people are not given as much to the habit of pondering problems as others are, but in the case of a person who practices judo seriously, even though ordinarily he may not be a very academic or thinking type, he will, if he gives himself half a chance, develop this habit of thinking about practical judo problems without too much effort. The reason why the ambitious judo player can tackle problems which concern his art, and do it without a great deal of effort, is because he can see the practical rewards inherent in the solution to problems which involve him in such a personal manner. And, as is well known to psychologists and educators, it is possible for even the most lazy and disinterested individual to act in an extremely energetic manner once he realizes that his hard work will result in some very great benefit to himself. Well, in the case of the judo player who treats his sport seriously, the personal satisfaction which he derives from making progress with his technique is such that he is forced to come to grips with the problems which he meets up with every time he goes on to the mat, because he realizes that if he makes no attempt to eliminate these problems, he will not make the progress which provides him with this personal satisfaction.

We can see therefore that in the case of those who practise seriously and who have a strong desire to make fast and genuine progress in judo, there is not much need really to remind them of the importance of thinking about the problems which arise during their practice sessions. Their ambition usually forces them to combine practising with thinking, as it were. However, what often happens, even with high-grade judo men, is that once they have knocked off the rough edges of a technique, as it were and feel that they have reached in its execution a reasonable stage of proficiency, they tend to be content with only practising this particular technique and almost give up treating it with the intellectual care hitherto given it. They take the attitude that once a reasonable stage of facility with a technique has been reached, there is no longer much need to give it much thought and that practice alone will bring about further progress. This is definitely the wrong attitude to adopt, because it is possible to be deceived by the attainment of reasonable skill into thinking that one has made much greater progress than one actually has. This causes people to stop thinking a great deal about a certain technique, when in most cases all they have done, when one realizes just what a judo technique can be developed into, is to scratch the surface of this technique. And it seems that, although progress can be made with a technique simply practising it against good opponents, once a man stops applying his mind to the problem of improving, no matter how slightly, the technique, he fails to develop his full potentiality as an expert in its execution.

And it is only by conscientiously practising the Seventh Principle on a deep level that you will ever develop true expertise in judo.

8 EIGHTH PRINCIPLE

As soon as you take up judo, start developing Counter Technique (Kaeshiwaza). But let it develop naturally. Do not be conscious of it to the extent that it interferes with your attacking technique.

To bring off counter technique against a powerful, experienced judo player is very difficult indeed. And unless one starts doing counter technique early in one's career, one never develops the naturalness in its execution without which it is almost impossible to have any success with it against high-grade judo men.

This being the case, it might be asked why therefore should one bother with using counter technique at all? Could one not have a successful judo career without bothering oneself with the time and effort it requires to become an expert in the art of countering the attempted techniques of one's opponent with the various techniques which can be used for this purpose?

The answer is that although there are many good judo players who do not have in their repertoire a very powerful counter technique, these men are usually very talented individuals who have exceptionally good judo skill, which skill enables them to do without counter technique. But even these men will be able to bring off counter techniques under certain circumstances even though they may not have great expertise in their execution. These individuals, the highly skilled type with an extraordinary aptitude for judo, are at the top of the judo scale, as it were, and can be said to be exceptions to any general rule.

At the other end of the scale, you find the type of person, who, because he lacks the energy and aggression to develop the positive forms of throwing technique, will rely mainly on counter technique in order to get the better of his opponents. And although, through concentrating on counter techniques he becomes very skilled in their application and therefore proves very often to be an awkward opponent, he does not as a rule develop into a great judo player. This is because in order to have consistent success in judo, one must constantly be taking the initiative. And this can only be done when one has a good repertoire of positive throwing techniques to use against one's opponents. Without this armoury, as it were, the counter specialist limits his chances of winning by the fact that in order to score against his opponent he first has to wait until they attack him. Which of course means that he is in the unfortunate position of not being able to control a contest by taking the initiative, which as we have already seen is essential to consistent success in judo contests.

Doubtless, the most rewarding repertoire to build up for the vast majority of judo players is the one which contains positive throwing technique, which will enable one to take the initiative in contests, and also counter technique, which will often deter your opponent from attacking you and therefore reduce your chances of being thrown by him. Without counter technique, your opponent will be able to attack you with impunity, knowing that the likelihood of his being counter thrown by you will be very small. And if he is also able to use counter technique skillfully himself, this fact will cause you to hesitate to attempt throwing techniques against him. And this also will increase the odds in favour of his beating you.

Apart from the fact that the ability to use counter technique is important as a deterrent to your opponent's attacking you with impunity, it also enables you to have a chance of defeating your opponent no matter what he may be doing, which is even more important an aspect of counter technique than the deterrent aspect. What is meant by this last sentence is that in judo, the ideal is to develop a repertoire of technique, strategy, etc. so that no matter how awkward, or unorthodox your opponent's grip, technique, stance, etc. may be, you will always be able to act in a way which will give you at least a reasonably good chance of beating him. Well, what happens when your opponent positions himself in the various ways possible in an attempt to throw you is that your relative positions become such that he is not only situated in a way which gives him a chance of throwing you, but he is also situated in a way which precludes your using many of the normal throwing techniques. You are therefore, if you want to be able to throw your opponent irrespective of your relative positions, compelled to develop effective counter technique. Failing to do this will mean that when you come up against a very lively, hard attacking opponent, you will be at a great disadvantage, due to the fact that most of the time he will be positioning himself for throwing you, which as we have just seen will also preclude your using many of the normal throwing techniques. Finally, in other words, unless you can do counter technique, and especially against the lively, aggressive individual just mentioned, you will finish up most of the time simply trying to prevent your opponents from throwing you, without having much opportunity yourself of applying point-scoring techniques, which obviously is not going to get you very far as a winning judo player. On the other hand, the practice and study of counter technique will enable you to achieve the ideal in judo, which is as we have already seen the ability to have a reasonable chance of beating your opponent no matter how he positions himself in relation to yourself.

9 NINTH PRINCIPLE

Develop a favourite throwing technique, which you must practise and think about more than the other techniques.

If there is one thing which judo men seem to agree upon it is the fact that it is absolutely essential for a person who wishes to get very far in judo to have a favourite throwing technique. And by this is meant a positive throwing technique as opposed to those techniques which are used almost solely as counter techniques. To be more clear, a positive throwing technique is one which you can use against an opponent without first waiting for him to attack you. A counter technique is one which you use after your opponent has attacked you. Of course it is important to have a favourite counter technique too, but this is not considered as important an asset as having a favourite positive throwing technique and will be dealt with in a separate article.

The beauty of form, and the speed, timing, and power of execution of the throwing technique of the top-class Japanese judo expert are undoubtedly the product of highly-concentrated specialization. The Japanese judo player will choose only one technique on which he will devote most of his practice periods. This does not mean that he will completely ignore the great variety of other techniques which judo contains. But he will definitely treat any of them as secondary in importance to his favourite technique. And he will make quite certain that any other technique which he spends time on, in addition to his favourite or pet technique, will be capable of being used in conjunction with or in support of this favourite technique. In other words, everything he practises will evolve from and revolve round his main throwing waza (technique).

Why it may well be asked is it so necessary to specialise in this way? Surely, this kind of specialization will tend to be so monotonous that one's enthusiasm for the sport will suffer? And what of the variety of technique in judo, is one not supposed to develop skill in a way which can be reconciled with this variety too? And so on. Theoretically, there are many different arguments which might seem to be a refutation of the belief that specialization is the best way for the judo player to become very good. The fact of the matter is, however, that when it comes to contesting with experienced judo players, you have no chance whatsoever of throwing them unless you use a technique which you have specialized in. Even then it is still a very difficult task. So how much more difficult will it be if you attempt to throw them with a technique which you have not specialized in?

The most convincing argument or school of thought against the school of thought which claims that the ideal way to progress in judo is via specialization is the one which advocates a variety of technique to be developed and then worked together in as subtle and strategic a manner as possible, bringing to bear on the technique the very roots of our intellectual faculties, as it were. And it must be said that this kind of judo can be quite fascinating, and especially so in the case of those players with keen intelligence and vivid imagination. And there is no question at all that the judo man who has become skilled in this type of fast, tricky, strategic kind of judo is a force to be reckoned with, especially the man who does techniques on both the right and the left. However, in spite of this, it has been the author's convinced opinion for many years that in the last analysis, the specialist will prove to be superior as a top class contest player.

The reason why it is necessary to spend such a lot of time practising your favourite technique is largely due to the tremendous importance of timing in judo. And if your timing is off, as it were, then throwing a strong opponent is out of the question. This point might be more easily grasped if we understand quite clearly what in judo is meant by timing. Timing is to be able to recognize an opportunity for bringing off a technique and then simultaneously to initiate a technique. Both of these ingredients constitute what we understand as timing. One without the other is like a bow without an arrow, quite without function. Some people are clever at recognizing opportunities but are unable to back this facility up with the simultaneous application of technique. Others, on the other hand, can initiate technique with no trouble, but they are no good at spotting the right opportunity for the application of the technique, and consequently finish up attacking at the wrong moment and of course failing with their technique. If any of these two types attempt to throw a strong opponent, they will always fail, due, as has already been said, to the tremendous importance of timing in the successful execution of a judo technique. Let us never forget that to throw a strong, experienced opponent is never easy to do, and if you have no timing, no matter how good your technique or how fast you apply it, you make it almost impossible. This is because once you give a person an opportunity to resist your technique and allow him to move his weight and power in the direction opposite to that which you are trying to take him with your technique, it is like attempting to throw a house and not a human being. Throwing technique, you see, can only be applied with success if you use it in the direction in which the opponent, at the time you attack him, has least resistance to your technique. Now, as the opponent is loathe to be thrown, and can easily resist your throw if you attack him at the wrong moment even with coordinated technique, or attack him at the right moment with poorly coordinated technique, you can see just how everything else is of little avail against experienced judo players if it is not backed up with timing.

All very interesting, but how does this justify or qualify the first sentence in the previous paragraph concerning the connection between specialization in technique and timing? Well, the truth of the matter is that unless a person specializes to a large extent, he will always have trouble with applying his technique with naturalness. In other words, he will always have trouble in applying his technique without having to be conscious of this technique. And unless you are able to apply technique with skill and power without distracting your concentration by being conscious of your technique, you will not be able to give all your attention to the problem of spotting and creating opportunities for the application of your technique. And if you are unable to do this, which is the main part of timing, you will have very little success with your technique. Specialization, therefore, enables you to build up technique to the point where you can use it powerfully and in a coordinated manner without having to think about the technique before you apply it at all. When you have reached this stage of skill via specialization, it is a comparatively easy thing to apply your technique with perfect timing. This is because firstly, your mind is free to concentrate on opportunities for throwing and leave your throwing technique to itself, as it were. And secondly, when you initiate your attack simultaneously with your spotting an opportunity, your technique will be applied with the tremendous coordination and naturalness which are the hallmark of specialized technique.

We can see therefore that concentrating on favourite technique as opposed to attempting to do everything in the book, as it were, will enable you eventually to apply your technique with timing, which as we now know is the ingredient in judo without which the judo player cannot hope to have much success when competing with clever, experienced opponents.

10 TENTH PRINCIPLE

Develop a special classical stance. And do not, unless under extreme circumstances, keep changing to other stances.

Success, or at least a feeling of success, must be constantly sought for in judo. The reason for this being that judo is a tough sport and like any tough activity it has the power to either make you or break you. And there is very little doubt that unless you take steps to insure your feeling that you are getting somewhere in other words achieving success, you could become one of those people who give up judo in a state of frustration and disenchantment. When asked why they have given up practising, they will often blame themselves by modestly confessing that they do not seem to have any aptitude for the art, or that their particular stature does not seem to lend itself very well to the correct execution of judo techniques, etc. Or, on the other hand, they will blame judo itself for their deciding to give up the practise of it. Conflicting statements like the following can be heard from different individuals of the latter category. "Oh, I am afraid it requires too much subtlety for me, I just don't have that kind of patience". Or, "The trouble with judo is that too much strength is involved, and it seems to me that spending one's time on a thing where strength is such an important factor is not being really artistic". And so on and so forth.

Now, none of the excuses which people make when they give up the practise of judo are seldom valid. To blame one's own stature is ridiculous because judo is unique in that no matter what your physique may be you still have an excellent chance of becoming a skillful and effective judo artist. To blame judo itself by saying that it either requires too much subtlety or too much strength is also incompatible with the consensus of opinion of most experienced judo men, because judo is what you make it, as it were, and can be an extremely subtle activity, or an activity in which strength plays a big part, or somewhere in between the two, etc.

Why then do some people who take up judo with such great enthusiasm and expectancy lose this wonderful enthusiasm and become disillusioned? There is no doubt in the writer's mind that the main reasons are only two in number. The first is that these people have had none or insufficient guidance as to the importance of adhering to commonly accepted judo principles. The second is that even though having been told of the existence of these principles and having also been exhorted by teachers and others to do judo according to these principles, they have instead practised judo the way they themselves think they ought to practise it and ignored the principles.

These people, due either to their ignorance of the existence of such principles or their inability to have any faith in them, never seem to do very well and consequently never feel the sense of success which we spoke of. This usually drives them to giving up the sport altogether. On the other hand the person who adheres to the principles of judo invariably experiences a sense of success, which leads him on to greater and greater things. And there are few experienced judo players who would argue against the principle that the development of a special classical stance is of great importance to the judo player.

Your stance will usually be determined by your method of holding your opponent's jacket, and your method of holding will usually be determined by your favourite throwing technique. So if your favourite technique is suitable for your particular physique, and your method of holding is suitable for your favourite technique, you should have no trouble at all in developing a perfectly natural stance from which you will be able effectively to do both of the things which a judo player must be able to do: to throw his opponent with especially his favourite technique, and to defend himself against all forms of technique.

The statement that from one stance a person can always have a good chance of bringing off his favourite technique and that he can always adequately defend himself from all forms of judo throwing techniques may strike many as a gross exaggeration. Its simplicity staggers the imagination. It is one of those statements that those without personal experience themselves seem quite unable to appreciate. It is however not a gross exaggeration but a simple statement of fact, which your own personal experience given the chance will allow you to eventually appreciate.

The simple truth of the matter is that in judo contest, the ability to concentrate and to apply techniques with perfect timing is so vitally important that anything which interferes with this ability must be avoided at all costs. And there is no question about it the inability to defend oneself against the opponent's throwing attempts in as simple a manner as is possible does interfere with this ability very much. And the simplest way to defend oneself adequately against any kind of throwing technique is simply to stay in the one stance all the time. You will find that if you do this all of the time, and not just some of the time, your body will, due to its being exposed to all of the judo throwing techniques again and again and again, gradually develop defence reflex actions against all forms of throwing attacks. And it will do this, if given the chance to develop in this way that is, in a very simple manner indeed, and not in a manner which will require on your part a large change of your body position, which change can cause such havoc with your concentration and timing. One can therefore easily imagine just how well one can get down to the business of concentrating all one's powers on throwing one's opponent once having developed this simple all-round defensive ability, which ability will more and more enable you to defend against the strongest of attacks without having to unduly interfere with your concentrating on attacking your opponent.

And although the development of a special stance is mainly to enable you to build up a strong and perfectly natural defence against every conceivable judo throwing technique, it is also to enable you to allow your attacking techniques to develop in as natural a manner as possible, because if your technique does not develop like this, you will never be able to use it with much effect against experienced judo men. Staying in the same stance all the time helps in developing naturalness in your technique because you can then initiate your techniques from exactly the same position every time you make an attack, which, because of the sameness of the action, reduces gradually your conscious awareness of the numerous little movements which constitute a judo technique. And the greater your power of doing techniques without actually having to think about them becomes the greater the naturalness of your skill becomes. Because after all naturalness simply means to be able to do something well without being consciously aware of it to the extent that this awareness interferes in any way with the desired effect of the action.

And in the case of judo technique, which technique when analysed into its elements is extremely complicated, the only way to develop this desired naturalness of skill is to do a certain technique in exactly the same way each time that you do it. This means that when you do a technique, your grip on your opponent's jacket should always be the same, the footwork which the technique involves should always be the same, the unbalancing actions which your hands make on your opponent should always be the same, the manner in which you secure the necessary leverage from your feet at the start of a technique should always be the same, etc., etc.

It is, however, not possible to do any of these things in exactly the same way unless you initiate a technique each time you do it from exactly the same stance. This means that the feet should always be in the same relative position to each other and as much as it is possible to do so the body should be kept in the same posture. What actual stance you will come to prefer is beside the point, what we want to stress is the importance of staying in it all of the time. If this is done, it will help you greatly to acquire the initiative in attack and also the confidence in defence which are the hallmarks of the successful judo player.

11 ELEVENTH PRINCIPLE

Think about theory, but never, for the sake of your judo progress and also for the sake of your personality, allow yourself to become a mere theorist.

This principle simply means that if you wish to become a skillful, effective judo player, it is necessary to practise. And this does not mean practise when you feel like practising, or practising once every two weeks, etc. It means that you must practise at least two to three times a week for periods from one to two hours per practise session.

It is no use however simply practising in a blind unthinking manner, because judo being what it is, a very complex physical activity, you must use your brains in pursuit of judo progress as well as using your body.

Some people may take this to be a contradiction, to a certain extent anyway, of the principle with which this article is concerned. This would be far from the truth. There is a vast difference between the practical thinking individual and the mere theorist.

The mere theorist for a start does not have much time for the practical results of his theorising; he treats activities, even obviously physical ones like judo, as mediums which provide him with the material for the quite pleasant activity of thinking. In other words, merely thinking about things is for him far more important than the achievement of practical results. And this really in a simple form anyway describes the mere theorist. And as he is not usually given to exerting himself much physically in judo, he seldom comes face to face with the stark reality of the truths of the art, and consequently never devotes his intellectual skills to the solving of problems the solution of which can be of tremendous practical value to the judo player. Instead, he passes the time, often too in quite an ecstatic state, posing problems usually of a very hypothetical nature and then attempting to resolve them.

Now, of course, there are many activities in which the theorist can do very well and contribute a great deal to the activity as a whole. Pure Mathematics is an obvious example of this kind of activity. Philosophy too lends itself to a great deal of hypothetical and abstract mental effort on the part of the person who engages in this probably the most ancient of all human activities. In fact, most of the activities which are usually described as academic are replete with opportunities for the theorist to find his niche. Whether he will ever become a man of wisdom is another question. I say this because it does seem that unless you concern yourself quite a lot with what actually happens in this life and not with what might or could happen or what you would like to see happen, then your chances of commanding respect as a wise man from other wise men are very limited. This is so because wisdom is concerned with truth and not merely cleverness and intelligence. And to reach a state where you are aware of the truths appertaining to a certain activity requires the following combination of things: a strong desire to be associated with only that which is the best, and the courage, strength, and decency to do everything in your power to achieve this.

In the activity which this book is dealing with, the one and only way to come to be able to execute the best technique, which is what judo is all about, and also to be able to teach the best technique with great conviction, is to practise judo techniques as frequently as possible and against competent and competitive opponents. And only on those practical problems which you constantly come face to face with during your practise sessions should you concern your intellect with. If you do this, your technical skill and your technical knowledge will improve at a most satisfactory rate, and your awareness of judo truths will as a consequence increase. If, however, you do not give yourself a chance to meet up with truth by regular, hard practise, but instead content yourself with the thousand and one hypothetical problems of judo, and practise only a little, your mastery of judo technique will be like the content of your system, negligible.

12 TWELFTH PRINCIPLE

Stick, unless circumstances and common sense do not permit, to a favourite grip.

All the methods of gripping in this article are for the right-hander. The left-hander should reverse the instruction.

Many things in combination contribute towards the complete make-up of the judo expert, and the elimination of any one of these things will of course have an adverse effect on his expertise. But the thing which does this most of all is the inability to fight for and secure a favourite grip. Because without that naturalness of movement when applying judo technique, whether offensive or defensive, which movement can only be used when he has developed a favourite grip, the effect of his technique on his opponent will be greatly diminished. And in the case of a powerful, experienced opponent, his chances of either succeeding with either offensive or defensive techniques will be almost nil.

The great stress which is placed on the importance of securing a favourite grip is often demonstrated in judo matches where the two players are of equal experience. Because it is when the experience of the players is equal, and especially when the securing of either party of his favourite grip would result in some sacrifice on the part of the other of his favourite grip, that one can easily see the fighting for grip that plays such a large part in modern-day judo contests. If the experience of the two players is unequal, however, then the more experienced party will often be easily recognized by his skill in easily securing his own favourite grip and by the ease with which he can easily render futile the attempts of his opponent to secure his own favourite grip. In fact, in the case of those judo players who have really mastered the art of gripping the opponent's jacket, they can, once they get their hands on their opponent's jacket, exert so much control over him that he is quite completely at their mercy and can be thrown all over the place with impunity. Not only that, but the opponent will find himself so tied up and controlled by this type that he will find it almost impossible to move, let alone attempt anything that could be described as an attacking movement.

The grip which you specialize in will depend on your physique, especially your height and your length of arm. In the main, the tall individual with longish arms will take a high grip with his right hand on the left lapel or collar of his opponent's jacket. With his left hand he will grip

31

the under part of his opponent's right sleeve as far up the opponent's arm as possible. In the case of really long-armed people, it is often advisable for them to grip even the back of the opponent's jacket just behind his upper arm at chest level.

Matsumoto of Tenri university, Japan, a great judo player, specialized in this grip when I was in Japan and had great success with it in contest. Although he received his judo training in Japan, he was actually a Korean, and this accounted for the fact that his arms were much longer than those of his Japanese opponents, whose arms are comparatively short. He had, therefore, like all non-Japanese who do judo training in Japan, to give a lot of serious thought to the problem of finding a grip to develop which would give him at least an even chance against his shorter-armed Japanese opponents, which shortness of arm, generally speaking anyway, gives them a distinct advantage over the long-armed foreigner. Matsumoto decided that the method of gripping with the left which has just been described would enable him to score against those with shorter arms than himself, because with it he could pull them in towards him and thus weaken their ability to resist with their arms, which is usually what happens when the short-armed man, who usually manages to gain the inside position with his hands on his opponent's jacket, is against a long-armed man. His right hand too would be thrust past his opponent's left collar to take a grip of the jacket a few inches down the opponent's back, thus enabling him to control the upper part of his opponent's body even more. This grip with both hands on the back of the opponent's jacket is certainly an extreme method of gripping, but very useful for those people with exceptionally long arms.

Of course not all very tall people grip in this fashion, because the grip of a player will be determined to a very large extent on the throwing techniques which he specializes in. Anton Geesink, the famous Dutch judo man who was the first non-Japanese to become the world's judo champion, is an extremely tall person with of course like all tall persons fairly long arms. But he specializes in gripping his opponent's left lapel fairly low down with his right hand, and with his left hand he grips his opponent's jacket near his right armpit. This grip, especially the fairly low hold on the left lapel with the right hand, is admittedly not a popular one with tall judo players in Japan, but as we know it certainly has paid great dividends for Geesink. One of the reasons why he has had such success with this grip is because the most effective throwing technique, especially during the last few years has been Tsurikomi-ashi with his right foot against the opponent's left ankle, and this particular throwing technique can be done with more power and ease with the fairly low grip on the opponent's left lapel with the right hand which Geesink prefers than with a high grip on the opponent's lapel, collar, or around the back of the jacket. However, although this grip fairly low down on the lapel does facilitate the execution of a technique like Tsurikomi-ashi, it is in the case of other techniques an obstacle to the natural execution of them. This of course can also be said of the high grip which Matsumoto of Tenri specializes in. His grip is advantageous for techniques like hip techniques where it is necessary to make a very deep entry with the hips against the opponent, but it is not a very good grip if you want to do techniques like Tsurikomi-ashi, Tai-otoshi, etc.

We can see therefore that it is possible to specialize in a grip which will enable you to execute certain techniques with tremendous effect but which grip will prove to be a liability when it comes to the execution of other techniques. Or, you can specialize in what is a more orthodox grip. The advantage of the orthodox grip is that it enables you to have a good chance of executing almost any technique with reasonable effect. And this is why it proves to be popular with quite a lot of good judo players. Mr. Sone, who was twice All Japan Champion and was also World Champion, is a tall man for a Japanese, but who is very orthodox in his manner of gripping. He grips with his right hand the opponent's left lapel neither low nor high, about chest level, and with his left hand he grips the under part of the right sleeve between the wrist and the elbow. And with this seemingly rather passive grip he can exert tremendous power via quite an assortment of techniques, particularly Uchi-mata, Osoto-gari, Hane-goshi, and Ouchi-gari.

What is important also is, once you have decided that a certain grip is suitable for you and in which you specialize, to study the different ways that you can quite easily vary the grip so that when on those occasions you find yourself against a player whose style, etc., makes it difficult for you to secure your favourite grip, you are not at a serious disadvantage. For example, once you have specialized in holding the right sleeve of the opponent's jacket with your left hand for some time, practise holding his jacket just in between his right shoulder and right lapel, or simply practise holding his right lapel. This latter hold is particularly useful against extreme left-handers who refuse to allow you to take your grip with your left hand on their right sleeve or shoulder or armpit region. When practising these variations with the left-hand hold, however, until you get used to doing them in conjunction with your favourite right-hand hold, stick to the latter.

Once you have got used to doing the gripping variations with the left hand in conjunction with your favourite right-hand hold, however, you can then go on to practising those right-hand gripping variations which could under certain circumstances prove very useful for you. What is a very good idea, once you have learnt how to fight for and secure your favourite right-hand grip with confidence, is to practise holding your opponent's lapel and collar at different levels, from the high position where you hold his collar behind his neck and gradually down at slightly lower level on his lapel to a point midway down his jacket. This very low grip is not of great value to the tall judo player from the point of view of attacking his opponent, but it can be quite useful for defence. Another variation of the right-hand grip which you should give some time to is to hold with your right hand that part of your opponent's jacket midway between his lapel and armpit. This grip is good for keeping the opponent away from you by pushing your fist into his body as he comes in for a throw. It is also good for pulling your opponent up when you attack him as opposed to pushing him up, which the lapel hold facilitates. This hold is also a good one for the technique Tsurikomi-ashi when you do it with your right foot against the opponent's left ankle. Another variation of the right hand hold and which has about the same advantages as the previous one is to hold the opponent's jacket at the loose part at the left armpit. Again, until you get used to doing these right-hand variations, do them with your favourite left-hand grip. Once you have accustomed yourself to doing them with your favourite left-hand grip, however, you should then go on to practise combining the different left and right-handed gripping variations which you have decided are suitable for you personally. Be warned, however, that these variations are only to enable you to handle exceptional circumstances, and are not meant as alternatives to your favourite grip.

As are the techniques which the short judo player specializes in different to those in which the tall judo player specializes in, so are the grips which he favours usually different to those which the tall judo player favours. The short judo player will usually take a fairly low hold on his opponent's left lapel with his right hand. And with his left hand he will take also a fairly low hold on the right under sleeve of his opponent.

The favourite variations of the right hand hold are simply to hold slightly higher up the lapel to about the height of the opponent's chest, or to hold even lower down the opponent's left lapel at a point just a few inches from the bottom of the jacket, or even to hold the very bottom of the corner of the jacket itself. And although it is a good idea for the small man too to get used a little to taking a high hold near the left collar area of the opponent with his right hand once he has developed a favourite grip, he will usually find that it is a rather risky hold for a short man to use against a tall man. This is due to the fact that in order to reach for the high hold he will have to stretch his body upwards to a large extent, which stretching action has a weakening effect on his ability to resist his opponent's throwing techniques. It is for this reason that it is absolutely necessary for a short man who takes a high hold on a tall opponent's collar to immediately effect a powerful drawing-down action with his right hand as soon as he secures his grip. This will make it much more difficult for the opponent to turn into him for a throw due to the forward and downward pull being exerted on the upper part of his body by the short man's right hand action. Another popular variation of the orthodox right-hand grip from the short man is for him to hold with his right hand his opponent's left under-sleeve. This enables him to execute Sode-tsuri-komi-goshi. It also enables him if he gets proficient with it to make it difficult for his opponent to secure a grip with his left hand.

The popular variations of the orthodox left-hand grip are simply to vary the height and position of the left-hand hold on the opponent's right sleeve. For example to hold the sleeve at the very tip instead of in between the opponent's elbow and wrist. This enables those who become good at it to throw effectively and also to prevent the opponents from taking their right-hand grip. Another popular spoiling grip, as it were, is to grip your opponent's right sleeve on the top with your left hand in such a way that you can exert downward pressure on your opponent's arm and prevent him from getting a grip on your jacket. This style of gripping was brought to the peak of perfection by Mr. Iwata, who is probably one of the greatest judo men Japan has ever produced. He is a short person and not too heavy but was capable of handling men far, far heavier and bigger than himself as though they were babies. He could do this not only because he had developed wonderfully powerful technique but also because he had given a great deal of his time to thinking about and practising the art of gripping. Very often he would, by taking the tips of both of his opponent's sleeves, prevent him from getting a grip with either of his hands, and then quite easily throw him with sode tsurikomigoshi.

Finally we come to the judo player of average height. And although, due to the fact that he meets constantly both those who are shorter than himself and those who are taller than himself he is unable to rely to the same extent as the short man and the tall man on one specialized grip, he must nevertheless by determination and intelligent thought endeavour to develop a specialized grip and stick to it as much as he possibly can.

From the writer's own personal experience, being of fairly average height himself, and also judging by the grip favoured by most Japanese judo players of average height, by far the most useful grip for those who are neither tall or short is what is called the classical judo grip, which grip you are taught when you start doing judo. This simply consists of gripping your opponent's left lapel just slightly lower than his collar bone with your right hand. And with your left hand you grip his under-left sleeve near his right elbow. If you persist with this grip, you can eventually use it with a very wide variety of techniques indeed.

Once you have specialized in this manner of holding to the point where it has become second nature for you to take this grip, then start giving some thought to the problem of varying your grip so that you will never be at a loss when you come up against those opponent's who because of their tallness or shortness, unorthodoxy, etc., make it impractical for you to stick to your favourite grip. If you come up against a very short person for example, you have no choice sometimes but to grip with your right hand the back of his collar. Or if you meet a very tall man, you will be wise often to lower your right hand grip further down on his left lapel so that you can use your right arm more freely and also avoid stretching your body up too much, which as we have already seen increases your vulnerability to being thrown. You will also, especially when you meet those who take up an extreme left-handed stance, have to get familiar with gripping the tip of the opponent's right sleeve instead of high up. This type will also very often force you to be satisfied with holding only his right lapel. Finally, once you have become skillful in doing techniques with your favourite grip on your opponent's right sleeve with your left hand, get used to holding under your opponent's right armpit and also in between his right upper arm and his lapel. These are variations to which you can easily adapt without disturbing your naturalness of movement to any great extent.

Above all, whatever your height, learn to fight for and secure your favourite grip. And only, if your experience tells you that you must, change it. You will soon be able to almost sense when this is imperative if you remain true to this principle.

13 THIRTEENTH PRINCIPLE

Develop an indifference to being thrown in Randori (Free Practice).

When engaging in a judo contest, whether it be a grading contest or a championship contest, you must avoid at all costs being thrown by your opponent. Because the object of engaging in judo contests is to win. If you do not have this object you are being neither fair to your opponent nor to yourself. In randori, however, the object is not to win at all costs, but to practise your judo technique so as to bring about an improvement in it.

Now, what is meant by improvement in judo technique is increased co-ordination of all the different actions which constitute a judo technique. This co-ordination is necessary to the development of natural, unthinking movement, without which, it is quite impossible to defeat an experienced opponent in contest. Improvement in technique in this sense may best be described as improvement in the application of technique. Because it is also possible to bring about an improvement in technique by actually changing the technique, that is by doing a certain thing in a different way.

Both of these kinds of improvement will result in what is known as skill. And this is what judo is concerned with. Because without a high degree of skill, the judo man is unable to defeat his opponents with that degree of power and effortlessness which is the hallmark of the true judo expert. In other words, although strength and weight do count in judo, the main thing to concern oneself with, if one would excel as a judo exponent, is the acquisition of skill.

Now, what is a traditional method of training for the purpose of acquiring this skill is randori or free practice. It simply consists of two judo players competing with each other in much the same way as happens in a judo contest, in that each tries to get the better of the other via the accepted judo technique, but without the degree of physical and emotional tension which is so characteristic of judo contest being permitted to enter into the proceedings. Because it is this tension, which I am sure all experienced judo men will agree is the thing which distinguishes judo contest from judo randori, which is believed to be a stumbling block to the acquisition of pure judo skill. Without this tension, it is definitely much easier to allow the body to act in the fairly relaxed and adaptable way in which one must act when doing judo techniques in order to gain co-ordination and naturalness of movement. The more spirited style of judo should be kept for the Shiai-jo (Contest Arena) and not for the Dojo (Practice Hall).

To eliminate the various kinds of tension which are natural to a competitive activity like Randori is, I am afraid however, much easier said than done. And it is an unfortunate fact that many people never eliminate this tension to any appreciable degree. What is very, very often the reason for this is our old friend pride. They just hate being thrown by their opponent, even though he may be a much higher grade than themselves. If the person they are practising with is a lower grade, then of course that they should allow this inferior individual to throw them is simply out of the question. For these people, every randori practice they engage in is a contest. They just cannot accept the fact that being thrown in randori is of no great significance, but that on the contrary, in their case anyway, it would no doubt do them a lot of good to be thrown more. Because it is just this determination not to be thrown at any cost even in randori that is responsible for the generating of too much tension, which as we have already stressed is fatal to acquisition of true skill.

What is necessary, therefore, when engaged in randori practice is to fight as though you meant it, as it were, but to endeavour to be fairly relaxed and not to concern yourself too much with being thrown. Because if you can develop this indifference to being thrown in randori, you will have gone a long way to bringing about that very special physical and psychological state in which your chances of acquiring real judo skill are greatest.

14 FOURTEENTH PRINCIPLE

Attempt to learn as much as possible from the advice and especially the example of good judo players.

The advice of an expert is invaluable. This is true of the judo expert as well as the expert or authority in any other field of endeavour. And if you are fortunate to be in a judo club where there are recognized judo experts as members whose advice on certain points you may receive from time to time, do not simply take the giving of this advice for granted. Because unless the expert is a paid teacher at the club, he is under no obligation to give advice at all. After all it has probably taken him years of effort to obtain the knowledge which he has, so if from the goodness of his heart he helps you in any way with advice, whether proffered or requested, make it apparent that you appreciate it.

And without a doubt, the most gratifying way to show a person who has given you advice that you really appreciate the advice is to put the advice into practice. So, if for example, you are given some advice on say a problem of gripping, do not just go away and be satisfied with yet another little addition to your store of theoretical knowledge, but instead, in your practice sessions endeavour for a reasonable period of time to use the advice given to you in a practical manner. Sometimes, you will discover, only after having given the advice a chance by testing it over a reasonable period of time mark you, that the advice in your own particular case is not of any great value. Then the thing to do is again to approach the expert with your problem who will then, if he has seen you attempting to use the advice he first gave you, be quite willing to look at the problem anew to see how the advice first given to you can be changed so as to adapt to your own particular style, shortcomings, etc.

The main thing, however, is to let a person who gives you advice see that you are sincerely interested in receiving advice because of the practical benefits that will accrue to you from it, and not simply because of curiosity, etc. And the best way, to repeat, is to let this person see you trying the advice out, as it were, when you are engaged in your judo training. If, on the other hand, he sees that you are not prepared by a reasonable application of effort and common sense to prove the value or otherwise of the advice, he will be loath to offer you any more. Because, as any person who has done judo for a long time knows, unless one attempts again and again in randori (free practice) to apply advice with confidence, one does not have much chance of proving whether the advice is any good or not. It is of no use at all simply attempting to apply it half-heartedly over a short period of time. So be prepared to treat the advice received from experienced judo players with the respect it deserves by doing what has been recommended here, and you will discover that advice can be quite invaluable to you. Take the value of advice for granted, however, and it will prove of little value to you at all.

What is very often taken for granted too is that all judo experts should be able to give advice on every aspect of judo. This to a large extent is true of very experienced teachers of judo who have also been proficient judo players too, and who over a period of years have analysed in detail every aspect of their art. However, it is not true of all judo experts, because many of them are not concerned with the teaching side of judo and consequently are not accustomed to habitually closely examining the kind of problem which besets those of less experience, skill, and talent then themselves. I remember asking Mr. Shinohara, who was captain of the judo team of Meiji university, which then was the leading university for judo in Japan, if he would teach me his Tsuri-komi-goshi. He told me that it was out of the question for him to teach it to me in detail because he had been doing it for so long that its execution had become for him second nature, and he was unaware in detail of what he actually did when he threw with it, which was very often indeed. I have no doubt that now he has taught judo for some years he would have no difficulty at all in describing in minute detail what actually he does when he throws with Tsuri-komi-goshi. It became more and more obvious to me however that even in Japan where people pay so much more attention to detail than we do, it was quite difficult for even top judo players to give you an accurate analysis of what actually happened when they did some judo technique.

What is absolutely necessary therefore if you wish to know how an expert does his technique is not only to get him to describe the technique for you to the best of his ability, but also, if you have the ability, to practise with him and also watch him carefully when he is practising with others. If you are not strong enough to actually practise with him then content yourself with observing his every little movement when he is engaged in randori or contest. If you get into the habit of being observant in this manner, you will often be able to tell an expert things about his technique which he probably did not realize actually happened. You will also be adhering to the latter half of the principle now being dealt with, which is to learn from the example of good judo players.

15 FIFTEENTH PRINCIPLE

Make it a rule to participate in as many contests as possible, grading and otherwise.

The road to real progress in judo according to the vast majority of Japanese judo masters is to train regularly in randori (free practice), do plenty of uchi-komi, and participate regularly in shiai (contest).

It seems that if any of these three main constituents of judo training are neglected to any extent, then to the same extent will a person's judo skill and knowledge suffer. There are of course differences in the degree to which each master or teacher will stress the importance of each of these three constituents, but you can be sure that with very, very few exceptions no teacher in Japan will ever eliminate completely from his system of training any one of them. And this is especially so in the case of contest, which is the anvil on which the sword of judo truth is forged.

In the early part of your judo training, your opportunities for contest experience will usually be limited to grading contests, your results in which will determine whether you will be promoted in grade or not. These as a rule are held every three months, so you have only four opportunities a year to test your judo skill under contest conditions. And this is quite sufficient contest work for a person in the first year or so of his judo training. Because during this period you should be concerning yourself mainly with the development of skillful technique, which can best be done by regular randori and uchikomi practice.

Participation in contest, more frequently, should be left until the second year of your training, as it is a well known and accepted fact that the nervous tension in an individual which is engendered by the contest atmosphere does in most cases compel the novice to resort to the use of just strength and aggression as a substitute for sound judo technique. Both strength and aggression do play a big part in judo contest, but only if they are applied in a scientific manner, which means that they should be applied via effective and well coordinated technique. And as it is very difficult for those who have not had sufficient time to develop their technique to the point where they can apply it under contest conditions, the very real danger for them if they take part in too many contests during the first year of their training, is that they will forsake the most effective and aesthetic style of judo, which is perfect technique supported by strength and aggression, for the less effective and ugly style of judo, which is nothing more than strength and aggression supported by inferior technique.

They make this choice due to the fact that they are not yet at a stage where they can possibly appreciate the very real value of perfect technique as a means of beating very strong and experienced judo men in contest, and also due to the unfortunate fact that, very often, beginners in judo can very often beat other beginners more easily by using strength and inferior technique than by attempting to use good technique. This is because in the case of beginners, the complexity of good technique does not enable them to apply it with the necessary speed and timing. However, if they persist in this maltreatment of the art of judo, which too frequent participation in contest too early on can result in, their chances of beating heavy, strong, experienced judo players, in contest, will be very limited indeed.

From what has already been said, it should not be difficult to see that the process of becoming a contest judo player who will be successful is a very gradual one indeed. We have already seen that too much contest at too early a stage of your technical development can result in your destroying your chances of becoming a good technician. What is worse, the tension which all beginners experience when going in for contest work, can, if they do too much, kill their enthusiasm and force them to give up judo altogether. Your second year in judo, however, if you have trained regularly and sensibly and given a lot of time and thought to the problem of improving your technique, should see you taking part in not only the grading contests, but also in any of the contests which are open to people of your own grade. People may not consciously be aware of it, but your first year in regular judo training not only lays a sound technical basis on which you can go from strength to strength technically, but it also toughens you up physically and mentally, which prepares you for the extra contest work of the second year. Which contest work, due to your improved skill and additional toughness, should gradually come to be for you a real source of excitement and personal satisfaction. Of course you will experience at first what is known as contest nerves, but with regular participation in contest you will overcome this and your confidence as a contest player will gradually increase. You should not overtax your enthusiasm however by doing too much contest work, and your main concern should still be with improving technically, which can, as we have already seen, best be accomplished by regular randori and uchikomi (technique repetition practice with a partner) training.

At the end of your second year in judo, if you have trained as recommended here, you will have developed fairly good and effective technique which you will be able to apply with confidence even under contest conditions. Your third year therefore will be the time when you should really pull out all the stops and hurl yourself into contest judo with the confidence and optimism which your two years of sensible training have given you. And as you should now be first dan grade, there will be many more opportunities to take part in contests than when you were a kyu grade. If you take advantage of these opportunities on every possible occasion, you will make great progress with your judo ability and knowledge. And if you couple this contest experience with regular randori and uchikomi practice, the day will soon arrive when you will find yourself competing in national and international matches against first-class judo players and with every chance of carrying off the honours.

16 SIXTEENTH PRINCIPLE

Start to practise as early as is practicable Kosotogari with the right foot and with only one hand, the right, against left-handers. If you are left-handed, then of course you will do it with the left foot and hold with only the left hand against right-handers.

If you wish to have an even chance of winning any contest no matter how unusual or unorthodox the techniques, stance, or grip of the opponent may be, then one of the things you must include in your repertoire is the one-handed kosotogari. Because, if you are a right-hander and cannot do this technique, you will when against a left-hander who can do it be at a serious disadvantage. And of course the left-hander who cannot do this technique will suffer from the same disadvantage when he has a right-handed opponent who can. In fact the left-hander, due to the fact that there are far fewer natural left-handers than there are right-handers, will have many more opportunities of developing skill with the one-handed kosotogari than will the right-hander. This is because the vast majority of his opponents will adopt a right-handed stance, which, from his own left-handed stance, provides a splendid opportunity for the application of the left one-handed kosotogari. Whereas the right-hander due to the fact that most of his opponents will stand in exactly the same way as himself will not find himself getting much practice in the application of this technique.

We can see, therefore, that the one-handed kosotogari, the vast majority of times anyway, depends for its success on the fact that the opponent is standing in an opposite stance to one's own. That is when you are in a right-handed stance and he is in a left-handed stance. We shall assume that the reader is a right-hander. If you are left-handed, then simply adapt the instructions to suit your left-handed stance.

What you must do when against a left-hander (and you intend to do this kosotogari) is to stand in an extreme right-handed stance. That is with your right side sidewards on to him. The reason for this is to prevent him from obtaining a grip on the left side of your jacket with his right hand. Move towards him in this manner when maneuvering to take your grip on his left collar or lapel with your right hand. He will also of course be in a position to take a grip on your right lapel or collar with his left hand. Now what usually happens at this point, unless your opponent can do the one-handed kosotogari on the left, is that he will attempt, in addition to holding the right side of your jacket with his left hand, to also take a hold on the left side of your jacket with his right hand. You can by practise become very efficient in preventing him from doing this. This is usually accomplished by pulling your left shoulder violently backwards each time he comes near to securing a grip with his right hand on the left side of your jacket, thus tearing your jacket away from his right hand. Actually this has the effect not only of preventing him from securing a grip with his right hand, but the action also pulls and stretches the muscles of his right arm, causing it to tire and ache and diminish in usefulness to him.

Now, if you persist in refusing to come to grips with your opponent in this fashion, which means that you should both have a double-handed grip on each other's jacket as this is the only way you can really do the vast majority of judo techniques, the referee will give you a warning, which if unheeded will be followed by a disqualification. However, and in this lies the beauty of the one-handed kosotogari, if you show that you can do positive judo even with only a one-handed grip on your opponent's jacket, then you can continue for quite a long time in preventing your opponent from taking a grip with his right hand, which means, of course, if you can and he cannot do the one-handed kosotogari, that he is at a serious disadvantage. However, the referee will be looking to see if you are capable of using this advantage by the use of powerful, point-scoring technique. If not, he will make you come to grips with your opponent.

So, once you have secured your grip with your right hand on your opponent's lapel or collar, and have positioned yourself so that your opponent can with only great difficulty grip the left side of your jacket with his right hand, if he is not as proficient in being able to control an opponent with one hand in this manner as you are, then the advantage which you already wield over him will increase.

Pulling him around in this way however is mainly to supply you with an opportunity for applying the one-handed kosotogari and not just to disturb his balance so much that he cannot use his strength. The opportunity you should be trying to create is to force him to react to his own rear after having pulled him forward. When this happens, place the sole of your right foot behind his left heel, and keeping the tension of the jacket controlling the upper part of his body with your right hand, change the forward pull on his jacket to an upward and backward push and reap his left foot away from under him, throwing him violently to his rear on to his back.

Occasionally, after you have developed this technique to the point where you can do it with great coordination of the different movements of hand and foot involved in its execution, you can actually sweep his foot away from beneath him in the ashi-barai style. This means that when you attack his left foot with your right foot, your timing is so good that there is no resistance at all to your foot action and he is thrown down on to his back effortlessly and with great speed.

What happens, usually however, is that you nearly always meet with resistance from his left leg which you are attacking with your right foot. So in order to throw your opponent with the one-handed kosotogari, it is necessary, even though you meet this kind of resistance, to keep up the pulling and pushing action with your right hand and to coordinate it with a determined and even prolonged repetition of the reaping action you make with your right foot against his left heel. The idea is to destroy his balance at two extreme points: at the upper part of the left side of his body and at the lower part of the left side of his body.

What characterizes the one-handed kosotogari, therefore, is the very great coordination required between your right hand action on the upper part of your opponent and the action of your right foot against his left heel and achilles tendon region. Also characteristic of this technique is the very real determination required to bring it off. So much so that, against strong opposition, one usually has no choice but to carry on with the technique to the point where you have to hurl yourself on to your back in order to combat the resistance put up by your opponent and throw him.

The most convincing proof of the very real effectiveness of the one-handed kosoto-gari I ever got was when I saw Hasagawa, one of the favourites, throw Koga, another favourite, with it in the All Japan Judo Championships. They were both left-handers, but because of Hasagawa's grip, Koga turned and stood in a right-handed stance. This proved to be his misdoing, because like a flash he was on his back for a full point. Hasagawa had thrown him with one hand, using the ashi bari style of foot action described above. For a man of koga's experience and skill to be thrown with this technique is without a doubt conclusive proof of its great usefulness to the judo player.

17 SEVENTEENTH PRINCIPLE

Until you are quite experienced, make your main grip the classical grip, i.e. right hand on opponent's left lapel and left hand on his right sleeve. (Left-handers take the opposite grip).

Although, as has been said in another article, you should specialize in a certain method of gripping, which will be determined usually by your height, this is in no way a refutation of the present principle. In fact, as was said in the other article, a man of average height would be well advised to specialize in the classical grip. But no matter what your height may be, you should, before you decide to specialize in a grip which is not the classical grip, stick to the latter until you can use it without having to be conscious about it.

This is much wiser than practising a non-classical grip for a long time and then going on to attempt to develop the classical grip. One reason for this is that the classical grip does definitely allow your arms and the rest of your body to move with a greater degree of freedom than the non-classical type of grip does. Which freedom of movement enables your body to adapt itself to the different movements and positions without strain or an undue reliance on one part of the body at the expense of general coordination. The other main reason for developing the classical grip before other grips is that it is much easier after having well familiarized oneself with the former to adapt to the latter than it is to do this in reverse.

Why many go on to use grips other than the classical at too early a stage is that they feel that the classical grip does not allow them to put to good use the full strength of the hands and the arms. And this is at first very true. However, one must never, ever forget that in judo in order to become really effective one should place technique before strength. This does not mean that the latter is unimportant, but it does mean that if you want to make best use of it, you should give technique pride of place. And if you persist with this sequence, you will soon find that the apparent disadvantages of the classical grip, such as the one above, are outweighed by the advantages.

One important advantage it has is that it is very difficult to prevent you from taking this grip. For example, when you study the alternative grips which it is possible to practise in the case of the right hand, you find that although they are undoubtedly scientifically sound, they do require more strength, ingenuity, and patience to secure and use than is the case with the right hand grip in the classical method. The same argument can be used in support of the left hand grip in the classical method. The classical grip therefore is easy to secure, and with constant practice can be used to execute a wide variety of techniques with real power.

Another advantage of the classical grip is that very often you will find that your opponent's stance, grip, height, etc. leave you no choice but to use this grip, or at least some slight variation of it. An obvious example of this is when you are against an extreme left-hander who is very good at gripping your left sleeve with speed. If you under these circumstances are unable to use the sleeve grip with your left hand, you will be in a position where you can offer very little in the way of positive attacking judo or strong defensive judo. In other words, you will be at the mercy of your opponent. Another type who often makes it imperative that you use the classical grip, especially with the right hand this time, is the right-hander with the nimble fingers who has your right sleeve in his left hand before you know what has happened. You will find that his facility with this grip and his nimbleness force you to take the classical right hand grip on his lapel. Any attempt to get higher than this or to get further across than this, say under his left armpit, is immediately nullified by his control over your right sleeve.

Another very important advantage in using the classical grip at first is to do with the very great importance of building up a natural and strong defence. And this can without a doubt best be built up via the use of this grip. Because much more so than many other methods of gripping it compels you to rely much more so not only on the arms for defence but also on the legs, hips, stomach, and chest. And in this way, you will find that with practice you can develop the kind of defensive reactions which will enable you to give all your concentration to attacking judo, which of course is the best road to the attainment of true judo skill and effectiveness.

18 EIGHTEENTH PRINCIPLE

In choosing your favourite technique, make certain that it is a major forward technique (Uchimata, Tsurikomigoshi, etc.) and not a rear technique (Osotogari, Ouchigari, etc.). Mark you, it is extremely important to be able to do rear techniques and also to be able to combine them with the forward techniques, but do not choose one as your main technique.

The main consideration in choosing a favourite or main technique is how easy is it to use techniques in the opposite direction when the opponent puts himself in an extremely defensive position and makes it almost impossible for you to have any success with your favourite technique.

This extremely defensive position if your opponent knows that you are a forward technique man consists of him using his arms in such a way as to prevent you from making the actions necessary to the execution of your techniques, such as body contact, entry, turn, etc., and also pulling you forward and retreating, which actions also render the execution of forward technique on your part extremely difficult.

If your opponent, on the other hand, knows that you specialize in a rear technique, such as throwing your opponent to his rear with Osotogari, and he decides to put himself in an extremely defensive position, he will most likely do the following. Using his hands and arms to prevent you from moving your body in too close to him, he will push you strongly to your rear by inclining his weight and moving his body forward, thrusting powerfully from the soles of his feet. He will also straighten and tense his legs backwards. All of these actions, forcing his body forward as they do, create a situation where techniques which rely on throwing him in the completely opposite direction to his rear are very difficult to do indeed.

Now the fact of the matter is that if you specialize in a forward technique, it is much easier, when your opponent adopts the extremely defensive position described above, to throw him backwards than it is if you specialize in a rear technique, to throw him forwards when he adopts the extremely defensive position described in the last paragraph. And this is the main reason why you should specialize in a forward technique in preference to a rear technique.

Another very important argument in support of this principle is that the major forward techniques require a more complex and subtle positioning of the body than do the major rear techniques. Major forward throwing techniques do therefore provide the judo player with greater opportunity for the development of coordination, agility, power, etc. than do the major rear throwing techniques.

And yet another very good reason for specializing in a major forward technique instead of a major rear technique is that most of the judo throwing techniques are forward techniques anyway and in the main have more in common with each other than do have the rear techniques. It is not difficult to appreciate therefore that if you specialize in a forward technique, you will, if you decide later on to start practising another forward technique too, be able easier to adapt to the new technique than will be the case if you specialize in a rear technique, which as we have seen do not resemble each other as much as the forward techniques resemble each other.

Of course the same argument in favour of specializing in a rear throwing technique can be advanced, in that if one becomes very skillful in one major throwing technique to the rear, then one can go on to adapt to other rear throwing techniques more easily than if you specialize in a major forward technique. But when opposed to the first two main arguments given above and the fact, as we have already pointed out in the third, that there are more forward throwing techniques than there are rear techniques, this argument cannot be considered a refutation of the principle expounded in this article.

19 NINETEENTH PRINCIPLE

Although defensive technique is extremely important, do not become a defensive judo player. Concentrate on attack.

As was pointed out to me some years ago by a good friend of mine, Chikashi Nakanishi, scholar and high-grade judo man of Waseda University in Tokyo, there are definitely two types of people in judo. One is the attacking type, and the other is the defensive type.

The attacking type is the person who has great difficulty in preventing himself from constantly taking the initiative and attempting to get the better of his opponent in as short a space of time as possible. And the defensive type is the more careful type of individual, lacking the initiative and aggression of the attacking type, and who is more concerned with not being beaten by his opponent than with actually beating his opponent.

Of course we cannot describe each judo player as either an extreme attacking type or as an extreme defensive type, although there are quite a lot of judo men who can be described in this manner. But there is a definite tendency for most players to go in varying degrees in either one direction or the other. And if you adhere to this principle, you will attempt to go in the direction of attack.

This principle, of course, like all of the principles in this book, must be used with a common-sense application. In the case of the principle being treated at present, this means, mainly anyway, that although there is this exhortation to concentrate on attack, you should not attack in a careless or too reckless a fashion, or attack so frequently that you become utterly exhausted, as this condition if experienced too often can exhaust your enthusiasm for judo altogether. Which would of course completely defeat the object of the principle.

However, if you use your intelligence when applying this principle, you will be giving yourself the best possible chance of developing as an effective and confident judo player with a good repertoire of technique which you will be able to apply with great naturalness.

This development will take place by sticking to this principle simply because you will find that by applying it you are forced to use your training time in the most efficient way possible. You will by attacking as frequently as possible be using your technique dozens and dozens of times in one training session, which frequent, and of course intelligent, repetition of movement is the only possible way to master the various complex and subtle techniques of judo. This habit of attacking your opponent with correct application of technique at every available opportunity will not only give you a much greater chance of mastering the various judo techniques, it will also develop in you reflex actions so sharp that your body will with time be able to react like a flash to any opportunity and take advantage of it with the appropriate technique. This type of reflex action is essential to the judo player, and definitely the best way for him to develop it so that he can react quickly enough to the various opportunities which he needs for the successful application of his techniques is to be an attacking judo player.

The defensive judo player, on the other hand, with his preoccupation with not being thrown, never attacks frequently enough, and consequently never really gives himself a chance to develop either his technique or his reflexes very widely. Of course, given time, he develops technique and reflex action to some extent. But he never attains to that advanced state of skill where he has a fairly wide repertoire of techniques, the centre point of which is a favourite technique. And unless a judo player develops this kind of repertoire, he will never be either much of a competitor or in later years much of a teacher.

20 TWENTIETH PRINCIPLE

Be a fighter. But on and off the mat, be a gentleman.

Judo being a martial art and because of the power required in the effective execution of its techniques, the judo player, if he is to have any chance of beating an equally graded opponent in a judo contest, has no choice but to release himself from the normal civilized inhibitions which usually influence his social behaviour and act in a very aggressive manner indeed. He must call upon all of his resources, mental, spiritual, emotional, and physical, to supply him with every bit of aggression in his being so that he can have a chance to achieve his very difficult object, the beating of an opponent as experienced and as skillful as himself. If he does not summon to his aid the total amount of aggression available to him, he knows from experience that he has no chance of beating an aggressive opponent whose sole object in the contest is to beat him.

There are of course, among those who take up judo, at one end of the scale the person who has a great deal of what is called natural aggression. That is, it requires very little effort on his part to express himself aggressively. This type of person, if he trains long enough and conscientiously enough to become technically competent, has a lot of success in contests. You must never forget, therefore, that aggressiveness, although essential to winning contests, is not much use in judo if you have not gone to the trouble of acquiring effective technique. However, technique unsupported by aggression, especially against experienced high-grade judo players, is also incomplete. Both are needed.

At the other end of the scale, we find the person who does not have an aggressive nature at all. This type of person is at a great disadvantage in contests if he just sits back and does nothing about his lack of aggression. And fortunately for him there is plenty he can do, but it requires on his part the ability to train hard and be ambitious. Because without ambition, hard training can be a very difficult thing indeed. But if he really overwhelms himself with the ambition to do well in contest judo, he will find that the hard, regular training he will be able to apply himself to as a result of this ambition will gradually bring out in him the latent aggression which lies within all of us; which aggression, if nurtured by continued hard training and regular participation in contest, will enable him to fight hard when competing and thus increase his chances greatly of becoming a successful judo player.

In between these two extremes of aggression, at one extreme the naturally aggressive person and at the other the non-aggressive person, lie in varying degrees the vast majority of those who practise judo. These people too, as in the case of the non-aggressive person but of course not to the same degree, must by hard training and discipline develop their aggressive potential, so that when competing in judo bouts they can support their technique and strategy with great fighting spirit. Because the fact of the matter is that if they meet a person in contest whose technical skill is as good as their own but who has more fighting spirit than themselves, the odds are on him beating them.

We can see therefore that one of the main objects of the judo man is to avail himself of all the methods available to him, hard training, self-discipline, etc., in order to develop in himself fighting-spirit. Because without fighting-spirit to support your technique, the latter will often fail you. This is true not only when participating in judo as a sport but is also true when using judo as a means of self-defence.

Finally, although the only way to do real justice to judo technique as a martial art is to support it with fighting-spirit, you will never become a great fighter unless you learn how to completely master this spirit and not let it control you. Because unjustified or reckless use of your fighting-spirit only diminishes its quantity and quality. However, if you learn how to harness it, and use it only when justified, it will increase in quantity and quality and when you actually have need of it, it will come to your aid with truly explosive force.

21 TWENTY-FIRST PRINCIPLE

Practise using the high grip, i.e. behind the opponent's neck, but do not specialize in it unless you are very tall with long arms.

One of the main advantages of the high grip is the speed with which you can take it. In other words, with the high grip, all you have to do in order to hold the opponent's jacket and therefore be in a position to control him is to slap your hand with a gripping action behind his neck, either gripping the collar, or the jacket further down his back. If you are right-handed then the hand which you use to secure this high grip will be your right hand, if you are left-handed then of course you must use your left. With your free hand you can take any of the grips normally taken with this hand, i.e. left hand can grip different parts of opponent's right sleeve, right lapel, part of the jacket between his upper right arm and his right lapel, etc.

The speed with which one can apply this hand grip, apart from its obvious advantages to the judo player when engaging in his art as a sport, also makes it an essential skill to those people interested in adapting their judo skill and power to self-defence situations where one simply does not have time or opportunity to avail oneself of those grips which although very strong once secured do take too much time to do so.

Another great advantage which this high grip has over the other grips which one can use with the right hand is that it enables you, once you have become practised in its use that is, to exert great pressure on the back of the neck and upper part of the back, thus controlling the upper part of the opponent's body and preventing him from making the movement necessary to his being able to attack or defend effectively. This is particularly so when he attempts those techniques which require that he turn his back on you.

What is another good reason for being able to use the high grip is that on those occasions when you come up against an opponent much shorter than yourself, you can always use this grip against him instead of using another grip which although generally may be more suited to your height and length of arm will however be quite difficult to secure against opponents shorter than yourself. And in fact it is for this latter reason more than any other that all judo players irrespective of height should get familiar by practice with the use of the high grip.

This however does not mean, unless your tallness and the fact that you have very long arms require that you should do so, that you should specialize in the high grip. Because, as we have seen, skill in its use will give a judo player certain definite advantages, the fact of the matter is that the high grip also has definite disadvantages. The main one is that it is almost impossible to execute certain important techniques if you hold your opponent behind his neck. The technique which it eliminates more completely than any other is Morote-seioinage, the execution of which requires you to hold your opponent's left lapel. It also, although to a lesser degree, makes the execution of Taiotoshi and Tsurikomigoshi very difficult. This is especially so against opponents who are much taller than oneself, due to the fact that these techniques depend on your being able to disturb your opponent's balance by exerting a strong upward pushing force on your opponent's jacket with your right hand. To be able to exert the necessary degree of pushing power it is necessary for the right arm to be bent to the correct degree. The bend in the arm is facilitated by holding your opponent's left lapel. The height at which you grip his lapel will of course be determined by your relative heights. The taller than you he is, the lower should be your right-hand hold. It can be seen therefore that the high hold against an opponent much taller than yourself will extend your right arm to such an extent that there will be insufficient bend in it to enable you to exert the necessary degree of upward pushing force required in Taiotoshi and Tsurikomigoshi.

These observations are mainly for the benefit of those individuals who are either short or of average height and who should be specializing in techniques like Morote-seioinage, Taiotoshi, or Tsurikomi-goshi. The same observations however are also valid for judo players who although not very tall are still too tall to specialize in techniques like Morote-seioinage or Tsurikomi-goshi and who will probably be specializing in Uchi-mata, harai-goshi, etc. This is so because although their techniques do not depend to the same extent on the powerful hand and arm force required in the first two techniques, they still need to be able to exert a lot of power via the hands. And the plain truth of the matter is that when they meet opponents taller than themselves they will find that the high hand hold behind the opponent's neck will not be of great value to them in this respect. They too, should lower their right hand grip and grip the opponent's left lapel, thereby enabling them to use their hand and arm strength to greater advantage via the upward and forward pushing power which this lower hold facilitates.

To sum up then, it has been stated that although all judo players should develop the high hold to a certain extent so that they can use it when the situation demands it when engaged in judo as a sport or for use as self defence, in the final analysis, because of the reasons given above, it is not advisable for those players who are not very tall to specialize in it. The only players who can specialize in the high hold behind the opponent's neck with advantage are the very tall players with long arms who very rarely compete with people who are taller than themselves. This is so because they will be doing techniques which are suitable for their height (Uchi-mate, harai-goshi, etc.), which can be done well with the high grip, and they will very, very seldom have to worry about meeting people taller than themselves in contest, which is as we have already seen the thing which makes the high grip impracticable to specialize in for the judo man who is not very tall. In other words, the very tall player using this grip can make full use of all the advantages which it offers without suffering from its disadvantages.

22 TWENTY-SECOND PRINCIPLE

Never change your favourite grip in contest unless your experience or common sense tells you that it is absolutely essential to do so.

It is safe to say quite categorically that a judo player has no chance of winning contests consistently unless he makes the effort necessary to developing a favourite grip that is suitable for his height, length of arm, and favourite throwing technique. And in the case of high grade contests, 4th Dan and above, a judo player without this favourite method of gripping his opponent's jacket when attempting to throw his opponent, or even when he is simply moving around the mat looking for and making opportunities, has almost no chance of winning contests at all.

And once having developed the skill necessary to your being able to secure your favourite grip, in spite of the numerous ways your opponents will use to prevent your doing so, and also once having developed your favourite grip to the point where you can, without conscious distracting thought, use it in the execution of your throwing techniques, the next object in your grip training is to practise with the object in mind of never, once having secured your favourite grip, being forced by your opponent to relinquish it and take another less awkward for him.

Just as there are many effective ways for an opponent, who is practised in these ways that is, to prevent you from securing your favourite grip in the first place, there are also many effective ways of forcing you to relinquish your favourite grip once having secured it. One favourite and most disconcerting method of doing this is for your opponent to simply pull his right shoulder violently and with speed to his own rear, supporting this action with a clockwise twist of his body. These combined actions will force you to release your left-hand grip on the right side of his jacket. If you are holding his sleeve, he will further reinforce the effect of the above-mentioned actions by dragging his right arm away out of your left hand. If on the other hand, he wishes to force you to relinquish your right-hand grip, he will simply perform the identical actions with the left side of his body. An artist in this method of spoiling is Kisaburo Watanabe, possibly the greatest stylist Japanese judo has ever produced, who became so good at it that it was almost impossible to lay your hands on him for more than a second or so at a time. And in fact, unless you had considerable experience against this method of spoiling, your hands and arms would be so exhausted by having their muscles and sinews stretched by this method of forcing you to relinquish your hold on his jacket that you were in no condition at all to use them to throw with. And of course this is what he was waiting for, because when he had reduced you to this pitiable state where your hands and arms were too weak and limp to use for either attack or defence, he would commence to go to work on you with quite an astonishing variety of techniques.

Against this type of opponent the problem of holding on with your grip is a great one, but it can be solved. However it cannot be solved without hard work, as is the case with most problems which face the judo player. The problem is one at first of developing hand and arm stamina, so that no matter how often you may be forced to relinquish your hold, your hands will never get so exhausted and weak that you will have to abandon all hope of securing it again and keeping it. And the only way to do this is to stick to your guns, as it were, whether it be in randori or contest and always make a determined effort to secure your grip and keep it. If your opponent forces you to give up your grip, you must take it again and again, and if you continue to do this no matter how often he may force you to release his jacket so that you will weaken and take another grip which will reduce your chances of beating him, your hands and arms will gradually develop great tolerance of the strain imposed upon them by his pulling his jacket out of your hands in such a sudden and violent manner time after time.

Of course, as has already been pointed out, there are many ways of making it very difficult for you to carry out this principle. But as the problem, to repeat, is largely one of developing hand and arm tolerance of the strain placed upon them by these methods, the best way to arrive at the point where you can put the principle into practice, is to persist with your securing and keeping your grip as has been recommended against the opponent who makes a point of pulling his jacket suddenly and violently out of your hands every time you manage to get your grip on it. There will be many times when you will sicken of fighting for grips, especially against an opponent skilled in fighting for his own grip and also skilled in fighting to prevent you from both securing your grip and holding on to it once having done so. You may at these times decide to forsake your favourite grip for another which might not prove to be so trying on the hands, etc. And although, as has been stated in another article, it is a good idea to be able to vary one's grip to a certain extent, the main thing for a person who would become a really strong judo player with great confidence against any type of opponent is to develop a favourite grip. And this can only be really done by making a determined effort to secure and hang on to your grip no matter what your opponent may do to prevent it. And once having developed by this determination what can be truly described as a specialized grip, you will have little difficulty in applying this principle.

23 TWENTY-THIRD PRINCIPLE

Beware of the advice and influence of people whose grade does not definitely prove that they have realistic and practical personal judo experience.

Judo truths can only be discovered or even appreciated via one method. And this method is simply to practise realistically as often as possible with as great a variety of opponents as possible. Now, this method can only be really satisfactorily practised in a fairly large club where you find a variety of styles and a variety of techniques being specialized in. However, even in small clubs, regular and intelligent practice can compensate to a large extent for the lack of variety in style and technique which one finds in clubs of this size. The fact of the matter is that even though you may have the good fortune of being a member of a large and famous judo club with good instruction always available and good players to watch practising or whether you may be a member of a small club with facilities in every respect leaving a lot to be desired, you have no choice if you wish to make any progress worthy of the name but to practise regularly and hard.

And there is no doubt about it, regular, hard practice is hard work, requiring as it does will power, physical exertion, and courage. This effort is recognized, however, by a qualification in the form of a judo grade being awarded to those who have made this effort by the appropriate governing body for judo. The grading system is based on the fact that human beings require some kind of incentive to make the effort necessary to making progress in an activity, incentive separate from the personal satisfaction to be derived from progress. Because in judo, which is a hard and difficult art to master, it has been realized that personal satisfaction is just not sufficient to make a person train as hard as it is necessary to train in order to make worthwhile advancement in the activity. A judo grade therefore, commanding respect as it does, provides a wonderful incentive to a judo player to get a grip of himself and get down to the task of getting to know his art, which to repeat can only be achieved by hard work. And the harder a judo enthusiast works the greater are his chances of being awarded a judo grade, for without the necessary training, he will have little chance of qualifying for a judo grade by defeating the necessary number of opponents in contest.

It can be seen therefore that a judo grade can be nothing but consistent with hard work and effort. In other words, if you work you can expect to attain to a high judo grade, if you do not work you cannot expect this. It is as simple as that. Because of this fact, it can be stated quite categorically that a person's judo grade is a direct indication or proof of the effort he has put into his judo training: the higher the grade the greater the proof of effort.

This latter fact combined with the fact that judo knowledge, skill, and an awareness of judo truths, to repeat, can only be gained by effort on the judo mat, proves quite conclusively that the only reliable people to seek advice from and be influenced by are those people who have proved their sincerity as truth seekers in judo by going to its greatest source of truth, the judo training mat, and thereby eventually qualifying for a judo high grade, the only proof of bona fide skill and knowledge.

24 TWENTY-FOURTH PRINCIPLE

Get familiar by practice and thought with the different parts of the sleeve which may be used for throwing and defensive purposes, i.e. tip, lower arm, elbow, upper arm, etc.

We shall assume in this article that the reader is a right-handed judo player. If he is left-handed, then he simply has to adapt what is written to his own case. The right hander, if he uses what can be called the basic judo method of holding his opponent's jacket, holds with his right hand his opponent's left lapel, and with his left hand, his opponent's right sleeve. The left-hander holds with his left hand his opponent's right lapel, and with his right hand, his opponent's left sleeve. What we shall be discussing in this article is the different ways one can purposefully hold one's opponent's sleeve for purposes of throwing, defence, or both. In other words we shall be concentrating on the use of the left hand when it is used to hold the opponent's right sleeve and not as can also be done when it is used to grip the opponent's right lapel, shoulder region, etc.

The first method of holding the opponent's left sleeve which a judo trainee should get used to is the basic method, which consists of taking with the left hand the seam of the sleeve under your opponent's right elbow. This hold is recommended for beginners and experienced players alike, allowing you as it does to get a grip with your left hand on the right side of your opponent's jacket with speed and very little trouble. Another point in its favour is that once you get used to this grip it enables you to execute with power a wide variety of judo throwing techniques.

Having got used to this basic method of holding your opponent's right sleeve with your left hand, the next spot on your opponent's sleeve which you should concentrate on is what is called the tip. This is right at the end of the seam of the sleeve near the opponent's right wrist. Now, although as can well be imagined, this hold with the left hand does not allow one to throw with as much power as other holds, it is absolutely essential to be able to use it, and not only for defensive or negative use but for the purpose of throwing one's opponent. And this is especially so when your opponent is a left hander who is skilled in using the tip of the sleeve. What happens is that he will with his right hand grasp the tip of your left sleeve. Now, if you can also use the tip of his right sleeve with confidence, there is no problem, because your position will be as advantageous for you as his is for him. However, if you cannot use the tip of the sleeve effectively, you will under these circumstances be at a serious disadvantage, due to the obvious fact that he is in a very positive position where he can make an attempt at throwing you, whereas you because you cannot use the tip of the sleeve cannot even make an attempt at throwing him. One might think that by simply giving a violent quick yanking action with the left arm he would be obliged to release his grip on the tip of your left sleeve. And of course this is what you have to do if you cannot use the tip of his sleeve for throwing purposes. But it is simply because so many of his opponents do this that the tip-of-the-sleeve specialist develops eventually tremendous tenacity in his grip and once he has the tip of your left sleeve in his right hand, it is an exceedingly difficult job to force him to relinquish it.

This particular grip, apart from the fact that with practise you can use it in the execution of various techniques on the right, is also used by people who practise the technique Sode-tsurikomi-goshi on the left, even though they are right-handers. I well remember Mr. Ito, a Japanese judo star of a few years ago from the famous judo college of Nichidai in Tokyo, who used to be an expert in the Sode-tsurikomi-goshi on the left. He would take up a right-handed stance and take a right-handed grip on his opponent's jacket with his left hand holding the tip of his opponent's right sleeve. This stance enabled him to do right kouchi-gari and right ouchi-gari which were his favourite techniques on the right. Very often, however, his opponent would, by resisting Ito's attempts to throw him with kouchi-gari, weaken his resistance to a forward attack. A second or so after this, Ito would have him on his back, having thrown him with left sode-tsurikomi-goshi. It must be said, however, that this particular technique although good for those judo players who are not tall, is quite a difficult one for the tall player to do with any consistency and therefore not the sort of technique which he should specialize in. In spite of this, it is an excellent technique to practise for the purpose of educating one's left hand in the use of the tip of the sleeve grip, depending as it does on the left hand pushing the right arm of the opponent forcefully up into the air. And it is this action which gradually gives greater strength and tenacity to your left hand when it holds the tip of your opponent's right sleeve.

There are advantages other than those mentioned up to here in being skillful in the use of the tip of the sleeve grip, but with intelligent experiment and regular practice these should become apparent to you.

When you have come to be able to use the basic grip near your opponent's right elbow and also to be able to use the tip of the sleeve grip effectively and with naturalness, you should then go on to practise using that part of the sleeve between your opponent's right elbow and shoulder. This is a good place on the opponent's sleeve to hold if he is shorter than yourself, enabling you as it does to pull him up with your left hand.

Another spot on the opponent's right sleeve which you should be able to use with your throwing techniques is between your opponent's right waist and his elbow, and under his arm. This is particularly good when you are against tall opponents as it enables you to hold the sleeve without extending your left arm too much, which of course is dangerous because it reduces the resistance which you can make against the strong pulling-upward action which tall people use against shorter people when applying technique.

Next we come to those methods of holding the sleeve on top of the arm and not below it. Starting with the part of the opponent's right sleeve nearest to his shoulder, simply dig the fingers of your left hand into the cloth of the jacket between his shoulder and elbow, and then inclining your body to your left slightly, bring to bear as much weight of your body as possible on his upper arm via a downward pulling action which you make with your left hand on his upper sleeve. This grip enables you to do a wide variety of throwing techniques and it also has the added advantage of killing to a large extent your opponent's right arm action. To have much success with this grip, however, requires a great deal of specialization, as a lot of practice is required in its use before the fingers of the left hand become strong enough to enable you to retain this grip in the face of the numerous very clever ways that have been devised to combat it.

Moving down the upper sleeve, we come to that part in between the elbow and the wrist of the opponent's right arm. This grip involves slapping your left hand on this part of the sleeve, clenching your hand firmly around the cloth of the sleeve, and then twisting your left hand with the sleeve firmly clenched in it down to the right side of your opponent's right arm. This grip, like the previous one, permits you to execute throws and also prohibits greatly the freedom of movement of your opponent's right arm, which of course plays havoc with his ability to execute throws. Again, as in the previous method of gripping, the finger and hand strength necessary to sustain this grip for the duration of a judo contest can only be developed by regular practising of the grip. There is no short cut.

Finally we come to the tip of the sleeve on the top of the opponent's right arm near his wrist. With the palm of your left hand facing downwards and the fingers pointing towards your opponent, grab the end of his right sleeve on top of his wrist and bear all your weight down on his right wrist via your left hand grip. This action if done before your opponent has a chance to take his right hand hold on your jacket prevents him from making throwing attempts against you, but you on the other hand can make throwing attempts against him. Which of course means that you have an advantage over him. The throws, however, which this type of grip will allow you to bring off are those which are most suited to the build of the short judo player. These are in the main in this case morote-seioinage, tsurikomi-goshi, tsurikomi-goshi on the right, and sode-tsurikomi-goshi on the left. And this is of course why the men who specialize in this type of grip are of short stature. It is also used by them when they have a points lead in a contest to frustrate the attempts of their opponents to get a grip on their jackets and thus waste time until the final bell rings. A master with this type of grip on the left sleeve when I was in Japan was Mr. Iwata who was only five feet four inches in height. Being a left-hander he used it mostly for left sode-tsurikomi-goshi. Often, he would hold both tips of his opponent's sleeves, effectively preventing his opponent from making good use of his own grip. This would very often have the effect of getting his opponent in a state not particularly conducive to cool, calculating action, which of course was what Iwata was waiting for, this all being part of his strategy. More likely than not, when this happened, the opponent would be hurled into the mat with one of Iwata's specialities. Often, too, to facilitate the execution of his sode-tsurikomi-goshi, he would wrap the top of the jacket at the tip of his opponent's right sleeve under his opponent's wrist, thus enabling him to push the wrist up from underneath which is the best way to use the hand action necessary to this technique.

Although, unless you are of short stature, you should not specialize in this type of gripping, it is still a very good idea to get used to doing it occasionally. This will enable you at least to have some idea as to how to handle the specialist in this grip when you come up against him, as there is no better way to get to know any weaknesses inherent in a technique or gripping method than by practising that technique or gripping method at least occasionally.

25 TWENTY-FIFTH PRINCIPLE

Develop a favourite hold-down (immobilization technique on the ground) into which you can easily get after throwing your opponent with your favourite throwing technique.

If you throw your opponent for a full point in contest, the contest is terminated and there is of course no need for newasa (groundwork). However, there are often occasions when you may be awarded only half a point for your throw due to its not fulfilling all the requirements for a full point. For example, you may have failed to turn your opponent completely on to his back, which complete turn is one of the basic requirements for a full point. Or, you may have actually turned your opponent completely on to his back, but have failed to throw him with the power which is expected in a true judo throw. In this case too you will not be awarded a full point, but perhaps you will be awarded a half point. And of course there are times when you may actually get your opponent to the ground with your throwing technique, but due to the reasons already given and others too, you will not be awarded even half a point for your throw.

It is under these circumstances, when you either get only half a point for a throw or nothing at all, that you must be prepared to continue the contest on the ground before your opponent has a chance to deprive you of the temporary advantage which your throwing technique has given you over him. And assuming that in most cases you will have thrown your opponent with your favourite technique, then what you must do is to give some thought as to what is the hold-down which you can most efficiently move into after being awarded only half a point or nothing at all after using your favourite technique. Because undoubtedly the best way to maintain your advantage over your opponent after getting him to the ground is to immobilize him on his back via one of the various immobilization techniques. And, as in the throwing techniques, you should develop a favourite on which you spend more time than you do on the others. Specialization, you see, is just as important in groundwork technique as it is in standing technique. And what could be more logical than to specialize in that hold-down into which you can most efficiently slide into after failing to score a full point with your favourite throwing technique, as this is the hold down naturally which you will most times have to depend on if you are to prevent your opponent from getting to his feet after having failed to score with your throw.

Once having decided what is to be your favourite hold-down, however, the thing is not to attempt to secure it only after you finish up in an ideal position for securing it, such as after having got your opponent to the ground via your favourite technique, although most times as we have already seen you will start from this position. What is absolutely essential if you are to build up a really powerful immobilization technique on the ground to the point where you can with confidence engage in groundwork with even those players who may be vastly superior to yourself in both weight and strength, is to be determined to fight for your favourite hold-down irrespective of the relative position of your opponent and yourself when engaged in groundwork. This means that although a relative position may lend itself more to your attempting to secure some hold-down other than your favourite, you should ignore this temptation to take the easy way out, as it were, and use your determination and ingenuity to gradually, little by little, improve your position with the object in mind of finally securing your favourite hold-down. Of course this is not an easy thing to do, especially against a determined opponent, but it is a wonderful way of getting to know the different constantly varying relative positions of your opponent and yourself which your body has to learn to adapt itself to in your pursuing of your object, the securing of your favourite hold-down.

26 TWENTY-SIXTH PRINCIPLE

Develop a favourite neckhold technique (Shime-waza). It should be one which more than the others can be worked in conjunction with your favourite hold-down technique.

Although neck-holds can be applied when your opponent and yourself are in a standing position, this is quite difficult to do even against people who are only fairly experienced. And even when engaged in groundwork, applying neck techniques against people who are experienced is no easy task. And unless you really apply yourself to the job of specializing in a particular neck hold, your chances of scoring points in a contest via this type of judo technique will be nil.

The reason why it is so important to specialize in the case of neck holds is because the application of them requires very great finger and hand strength, and it seems that the only way to create this strength is by practising the neck holds themselves. Of course, exercises designed to develop hand strength can do nothing but good, but these alone are inadequate, as the strain imposed upon the fingers, hands, and arms in the process of securing a neck lock against a strong opponent is the kind which cannot be got from exercises.

How then does one decide on the particular neck lock which one should specialize in? As in the case of deciding which hold-down to specialize in, our decision was determined by choosing one which we could use very well with our favourite throwing technique (see twenty-fifth principle), so when deciding which neck-hold to specialize in, we must pick one which will work well in conjunction with our favourite hold-down technique.

Using this as the basis for our choice will easily be appreciated when it is realized that before you can start to contemplate applying a neck lock, it is at first absolutely necessary to control your opponent with your body, legs, etc. (we naturally assume that the opponent is strong and experienced). If you attempt to go straight for a neck-lock before bringing your opponent under your control, you will find that he will easily be able to escape your attempts and get to his feet. And what better way of controlling your opponent on the ground than with the hold-down technique which you practise more than any other: your speciality.

The fact of the matter is that the vast majority of points which are scored in groundwork in contest are for hold-down techniques, simply because they are easier to do than are the neck locks or the arm locks, which are the other means of scoring points in judo groundwork. However, in his attempts either to prevent you from applying a hold-down technique or to extricate himself once you have applied one, your opponent may give you an opportunity to apply a neck-lock. This opportunity can be given when your opponent shifts his hands and arms from near his neck and throat, which is the best place for them to be if he wishes to defend against neck locks, in order to use them to force some part of your body away from him and weaken your control over him. Or it may be given when, as so often happens, he manages to escape from the position where he is being held on his back, which position is necessary before a hold-down is called, by turning over on to his stomach or on to all-fours. This position gives you an opportunity to apply a neck-hold technique from his rear such as kataha-jime, okuri-eri-jime, etc.

Knowing of these opportunities and others is of course of very little value if you cannot by skillful and aggressive movement take advantage of them. And the best way to get to be able to take advantage of them is to base your groundwork on the fact that you will have very little chance of getting the better of your opponent by neck-locks unless you learn first to control him on the ground with your body in such a way that he will not be able to get to his feet. And as most of the time you will be exerting this control, at the outset of a groundwork encounter anyway, with your favourite hold-down, you will gradually by practice realize just what kind of opportunities this presents.

27 TWENTY-SEVENTH PRINCIPLE

If you are of medium height, develop one technique which is effective against short men, and another which is effective against tall men. For example, develop uchi-mata in the first case, and morote-seoinage in the second.

If you are a very tall person, then all you need to do so that you will have a good chance of winning your contests, is to specialize in one of those throwing techniques which are known to be effective against players shorter than oneself. And the one which, by a very large consensus of opinion in judo circles, is thought to be the most effective against players shorter than oneself is uchi-mata. Anton Geesink, for example, for years beat all of his opponents without hardly ever having to resort to any other technique but this.

The very short judo player too can rely to a very great extent on one special throwing technique for the purpose of winning contests. As the vast majority of his opponents will be taller than himself, all he has to do is to plug away, as it were, at one of those techniques which are proved to be effective against players much taller than oneself. And the technique which in the main is preferred by the short judo man is morote-seoinage. Pariset, for example, the great French judo man and the only man to take the title of European Judo Champion from Geesink, being a short man used morote-seoinage with great effect during his very successful judo career.

The judo player of medium height, however, due to the fact that he will constantly meet, in contest, players who are taller than himself, players who are shorter than himself, and also players who are the same height as himself, cannot afford to depend on only one major throwing technique in order to win his contests. He must as it were, split his attention and concentrate on two major throwing techniques. One of these must be a technique which is known to be effective against men shorter than oneself, and the other must be a technique which is effective against men taller than oneself.

The technique which you should develop so that you will always have a reasonable chance against people shorter than yourself is uchi-mata. This is undoubtedly the most widely used forward throwing technique against players shorter than oneself in judo today. Osoto-gari is the most widely used rear throwing technique against players shorter than oneself, but as it is more advisable to specialize in major techniques which are forward techniques than which are rear techniques, we shall not consider it in this article as a technique suitable for specialization (see eighteenth principle). This does not mean, however, that you should not consider osoto-gari as being an essential technique for your judo repertoire. The uchi-mata technique, once developed, is also a technique with which you can throw opponents who are the same height as yourself and also slightly taller. It can also be used on occasions to throw opponents who are much taller than oneself. For example, this is possible if your tall opponent bends forward. Koga, famous judo star of recent years, could do this with his uchi-mata, but he had the advantage of being a left-hander, and was very talented with an excellent contest temperament as well. However, when he met Anton Geesink, also an uchi-mata specialist, in the third world judo championships in Paris in 1960, Geesink beat him with right uchi-mata. The main reason why he did so was that although both men had perfect uchi-mata techniques, Geesink had the advantage of being much taller than Koga and was therefore able to use his uchi-mata with greater effect than was Koga.

When it comes to choosing a major forward technique to develop so that you can use it to throw those opponents who are much taller than yourself, the choice, being wider, is therefore not so simple as in the case of choosing the best technique for use against players shorter than yourself. The main techniques used for this purpose are morote-seoinage, tsurikomi-goshi, tai-otoshi, and ippon-seoinage. All of these techniques if developed will enable you to throw opponents much taller than yourself. However, if your opponent through experience has developed powers of resistance to these techniques, then the one amongst them which will give you the most chance to throw him consistently is morote-seoinage.

This, however, unless you are very short and your opponent tall, is a difficult technique to do perfectly. By which is meant that your right hand (the one holding your opponent's left lapel) must be swung across your opponent's front so that your right elbow can be pushed right across the front of his chest to the right side of it. This position of the right hand and arm enables you to get your body well underneath your opponent and well across to his right, enabling you to gain firm control over the upper part of his body so that he cannot escape your throwing action, which is done mainly with the hands and arms.

If, however, the disparity in your respective heights is not great enough to enable you to do the morote-seoinage in this perfect manner, or if the fact that your arms may be too long to enable you to position yourself perfectly, then you must do the style of morote-seoinage which is somewhere between the perfect method just described and tsurikomi-goshi.

In this style of morote-seoinage, the right arm is not pushed as far across the opponent's chest as in the perfect method, nor is it positioned as far to the left of the opponent's chest as is the case with tsurikomi-goshi: it is positioned at a point in between these two extremes. This method is used a great deal by Japanese judo players and is often referred to as tsurikomi-goshi. The fact of the matter is it is neither the classical form of tsurikomi-goshi nor the classical form of morote-seoinage, but a compromise between the two.

Finally, what you must give a great deal of thought to if you are of medium height and are developing two major forward techniques with which you can throw those players taller than yourself and those shorter than yourself, is the problem of how to grip your opponent's jacket, especially with regard to your right hand hold. Broadly speaking you have two courses open to you.

The first one is to develop a grip which will enable you without changing it to do both techniques of your choice. This grip would involve gripping your opponent's left lapel not too low down nor too high up. This grip with your right hand will enable you with practice to do your two techniques effectively. It is only with practice, however, that you will find just the right spot to hold on your opponent's left lapel which will suit you personally. To a great extent what will determine your choice of grip height on the lapel will be the length of your right arm. This is always a main consideration in the case of problems concerning one's grip. If you decide that the course outlined here is the one for you, you must be prepared if you are to succeed with it, to fight with great determination to secure the grip of your choice no matter what your opponent may do to attempt to prevent it. With this kind of determination supported with perseverance, your body and techniques will gradually mould themselves to your grip and you will be well on your way to all-round ability from the point of view of being able to handle opponents of any height.

The other course open to you is to specialize in one grip for one of your techniques, and also to specialize in another grip to use with your other main technique. For example, when against opponents shorter than yourself whom you will attempt to throw with, say, uchi-mata, then you take with your right hand a high hold on your opponent's left collar, being as it is an easy hold to secure against smaller players and also a hold with which uchi-mata can be done effectively. On the other hand, if you meet up against an opponent taller than yourself against who you will use, say, your morote-seoinage, then in this case a high hold on his left collar with your right hand would not be suitable for your intended technique. You, therefore, take a hold further down his left lapel with your right hand, which hold lends itself to your throwing your opponent with your intended technique and also enables you to use your right hand more effectively for purposes of defence against a tall opponent.

This latter course is not as good for the determined aggressive judo player as is the first course, but it certainly does have a great deal of merit. For one thing it is very useful when against short left-handed judo players if you yourself are right-handed, and of course vice versa, when it is very difficult to secure anything but a high grip on the opponent's collar. It also forces you to learn the high grip which is very important.

28 TWENTY-EIGHTH PRINCIPLE

Learn to control your opponent by pushing him backwards.

The main object in pushing your opponent backwards is to induce him to resist your push by pushing his weight in your direction. When he does this you have a good opportunity to execute a forward throwing technique by taking advantage of the fact that his body, at the moment he resists your push by inclining his body towards you, is actually losing its balance in the direction it goes when thrown forward. The difficult thing, however, is to take advantage of this momentarily inclining of your opponent's body forward. And this can only be done effectively and with the necessary speed by, of course, being ready for your opponent's forward reaction to your push, and also correct positioning of your feet, so that you can move smoothly and powerfully into your throwing technique before he has time to see what is happening and to act accordingly. Acting accordingly means, of course, that he will resist your forward throw by pulling the top of his body violently to his rear and pushing the lower part of his body (hips, thighs, etc.) strongly forward, which concerted actions render a forward throwing action on your part out of the question. If, however, you can manage to get your throw started before he has time to put up this resistance, the fact that he was already heading in the direction of your throw when you started it will add tremendous power indeed to your throw. In fact if you can manage to trick a person without a great deal of experience in this manner, you find that he is absolutely hurled on to the mat with great force without your having felt any strain or effort at all in executing the throw. However, to trick experienced players in this way is another kettle of fish altogether. But with practice and the application of your common sense so that your footwork will enable you to move swiftly and efficiently into your throw when your opponent resists your push, you will eventually be able to use this push-throw method against anybody.

The greatest exponent of this method out of the great number of judo men I practised with during my stay in Japan was Mr. Kawano, the Japanese Police Champion. I believe he was forced to get skillful with it so that he would not meet up with too much resistance when coming in for his favourite throwing technique, tsurikomi-goshi. He was, you see, rather tall for a tsurikomi-goshi specialist and couldn't afford to have his opponent resisting when he turned into him with his speciality. But with his very skillful and clever way of pushing his opponent backwards, he was able to reduce the resistance to his tsurikomi-goshi by forcing his opponents to react forward, which enabled him to put his speciality to very good use indeed.

What is also necessary in judo is to be able to control your opponent so that he has difficulty in concentrating on what he intends to do, which in standing technique (tachi-waza) is to throw you, or of course to prevent you from throwing him. When he is best able to give the maximum concentration to these objects is when he is standing in his favourite stance and not being distracted by too much movement either on his own part or on your part. And what is done in judo a great deal to disturb your opponent's concentration is to force him to move out of his solid favourite stance in which he is most dangerous by pushing him backwards. Of course this movement will also distract you as much as it will him, so what one may ask is there to be gained by it? The fact is that if he is as good at controlling you by pushing as you are at controlling him by pushing, then of course a stale mate will result and neither of you will be able to gain much advantage over the other. However, if you are stronger and cleverer at controlling your opponent by pushing than he is of controlling you by pushing, then even if you do also distract your attention by pushing as well as distracting his, this distraction will not affect your ability to throw and defend as much as it will affect his. This is due to the fact that you have greater experience in finding yourself in such circumstances than he has, and are therefore not as greatly disturbed by them. In other words your experience enables you to adapt to the dynamic situations which result when you push your opponent forward. Which means, as Mr. Kawano could do so brilliantly with his pushing technique, that you can domineer a contest by constantly creating a situation where your opponent cannot concentrate sufficiently to be effective but where you can.

29 TWENTY-NINTH PRINCIPLE

Learn to control your opponent by pulling him forwards.

If you engage in a judo contest with a person who is clever and powerful with it at forcing you to come constantly forwards by himself retreating and pulling you with his hands on your jacket, you will, unless of course you can do the same thing to him, find yourself to a great extent domineered by him. You will find for example that you are so occupied with the thought of keeping a strongly balanced posture due to being pulled forward all of the time that you cannot give the necessary degree of concentration to your main object, which is that of throwing your opponent forcefully to the ground. We realize of course that in judo we are advised to go forward if our opponent pulls us and to go back if our opponent pushes us. And this also we must practise doing as an essential part of our judo training, because if often happens that due to the speed, cleverness, or suddenness of our opponent's maneuvers we have no alternative but to go in the direction we are pulled or pushed so that we can preserve most efficiently our equilibrium. If, however, you come up against a specialist in the art of controlling his opponent by forcing him to come forwards against his wishes, you will find that his experience in his pulling style, as it were, enables him to domineer the contest and of course make himself favourite to win. In other words, simply coming forward a little bit faster than he pulls you, as you are advised to do generally, is not the answer to this type of individual. And in modern-day judo there are many such individuals.

What you must do is also, by practice and intelligent thought, get to know how to control your opponent by pulling him forwards, so that you can by your knowledge and skill domineer the contest when against a player who has ignored this part of his training, and more important still so that you can at least have an equal chance when against a player who also favours this dynamic kind of maneuvering. What often happens too when two players both clever at disturbing their opponent's concentration and balance by keeping him moving forwards, meet in a contest, is that they, by tacit mutual consent, refrain from attempting to gain some advantage over each by trying to force each other forwards, knowing that as they are both as clever as each other in doing this, that if they attempted it, only a stale mate would result. But at least it gives both men an equal chance of throwing each other in the contest, which fact indicates the importance very often of being able to do something even if you do not attempt to do it. We can see therefore that the best way to guarantee that you will not be pulled all over the place by an opponent who favours this kind of strategy is to make it very clear to him by your actions that you too can dish out the same medicine, as it were.

.

30 THIRTIETH PRINCIPLE

Learn most of all to control your opponent with your hands and arms.

The ideal thing to aim for in judo with reference to the use of the hands and arms, is to employ them in such a way that you can take a grip on your opponent's jacket which can be used effectively with your throwing technique and which will also enable you to prevent your opponent from securing a grip on your jacket secure enough and strong enough to allow him to use it for either purposes of attack or defence.

Needless to say, to be able to employ the hands and arms in this perfect manner requires knowledge and a great deal of practice. The initial knowledge will of course have to come from a competent teacher of judo. What is required then of you is that you put this instruction into practice against opponents who are also attempting to control you with their arms and hands. Regular practice against this type of opponent will raise a number of problems which you would never have thought of without this kind of practice. You will for example practise with people whose own method of gripping makes it extremely difficult for you to take even a reasonably strong grip on their jackets let alone control them with your hands and arms. But this is the only sort of experience that will enable you to gain the knowledge and skill necessary to your development, because you are being forced to get down to the job of applying your intelligence to the problem. And it is just this combination of practice and application of intelligence to the problems which your practice raises that will eventually make you competent to handle even the most skillful or awkward of players in the area of hand and arm control.

Now what you must be on your guard against when trying to implement this principle, is making the very common mistake of thinking that it involves your constantly changing your method of gripping your opponent's jacket every few seconds or so with the object of confusing him and also bettering your hand position. This is a beginner's mistake, which is usually eradicated as he gets more experienced, but which can lead to people giving up judo before they get this experience due to the fact that this constant changing of the hand grip is definitely not a good way to become skillful either in attacking or defensive technique and leads to frustration and a sense of failure (see twelfth principle). However, in the process of developing a favourite grip, you will from time to time, in the light of that which your experience tells you, find that you will have to make slight and sometimes even big changes in your manner of gripping. And then, in the light of further experience, you may even decide to go back to your former grip. Everybody who attempts to do anything difficult goes through this process, which is simply the process of learning.

Once having developed a favourite effective grip with which you can use your attacking techniques, you should then make it a point of using the same grip for the purpose of domineering your opponent's every move, whether it be offensive or defensive. What should be practised, for example, is, without changing your hand position on your opponent's jacket, pull your right hand forward, upward, and outward, pushing his left arm away with your own right forearm. This has the effect of weakening his left hand hold on your jacket, which of course eliminates quite effectively his chances of using this hand and arm strongly for either purposes of attack or defence. This method of controlling your opponent's arm is particularly effective against opponents who with their left hand hold your jacket near the front or thereabouts of your right shoulder region, or against left-handers who take a high hold with their left hand on your collar or lapel. If, on the other hand, you take a rather high hold with your right hand, and your opponent's left hand hold is lower than your right hand hold, this method cannot be used by you. What you must do in this case is to pull your right elbow across to your left, force it down in between your opponent and yourself, and then force it backwards to your own rear and out to your own right. This again has the effect of weakening his left hand grip. This method will often require you to bend your body forward and down so as to manipulate your right elbow properly. It must be remembered that you do not release your right hand hold on your opponent's jacket while you are working your arm in the manner described. Another method used with the object of weakening your opponent's grip is to pull him towards you with your right hand while at the same time pushing the right front or side of your chest against his left arm. This is useful against those people who push their left hand like a ramrod into your chest.

These few examples will give you a clear idea of what is meant by this principle, and with regular application of the principle your effectiveness as a contest judo player will increase tremendously.

31 THIRTY-FIRST PRINCIPLE

Never butt, but make full use of the head both in standing judo and groundwork.

The head also includes the different parts of the face which can be used without running the risk of injury to them, such as the chin, jaw, cheek bones, etc.

What strikes one as surprising when watching judo contests in Japan for the first time, and particularly in the lively, dynamic contests between university students, is the fact that both contestants when maneuvering for an advantage very often position themselves so that the forehead of each is pressed firmly against that of the other. This position is reminiscent of the position taken up by two stags when engaged in combat. The reason why they use their forehead in this fashion is to enable them more easily to position their arms inside their opponent's, which arm position gives them a distinct advantage from the point of view of attack and also defence. What happens is that in the attempt to secure the inside position with the hands and arms, each man in order to foil the other's attempts finds that he has to bend his body lower and lower and also try to get his head beneath his opponent's. This results usually in both men being bent, right over, their arms almost touching the mat, and with their heads very low with their foreheads stuck together, each trying little by little to get his head slightly lower than the other's in a desperate attempt to get the inside position with the hands and arms. In other words, regarding either getting a great advantage over the other by getting his head much lower than the other's and consequently getting the inside position with the hands and arms, a stale mate usually results. This is because both men are usually equally skillful in attempting to secure an advantage in this particular manner. This does not mean however that some advantage is never gained by one side or the other, and it is this even slight advantage which can often result in victory instead of defeat for the person clever and determined enough to gain it.

Another way to put the head to good use in standing judo is when up against the tall judo player who with his right hand takes a high grip on your left collar. When this happens, you swiftly slip your head under his right wrist so that he finishes up with both of his hands on the right side of your jacket, which grip makes it difficult for him to throw you. This move is very useful against the tall man who grips high and who you know is not skilful at throwing when both his hands are on the right side of your jacket. However, some tall men can throw very effectively even when their hands are positioned in this way, and in their case it is better not to use this move.

Mr. Ito, the famous judo player of the Japanese police who was six feet five inches tall, could throw very powerfully with this grip, and one year in the All Japan Championships almost beat the champion Inokuma with O-Soto-Gari done with this grip after Inokuma slipped his head beneath Ito's right wrist. The moral here is 'Know Your Opponent'.

The above two examples will give you some idea as to what is meant by this principle when applied to standing judo and with experimentation you should have no difficulty in discovering other useful ways of using the head.

In groundwork also, efficient use of the head can enhance greatly your effectiveness when engaging in judo on the ground. It's more obvious uses can be seen in immobilization techniques like kata-gatame and tate-shiho-gatame, where one uses the head to trap the opponent's arm and head in between your own arm and head, and in arm locks like ude-gatame, where the head controls the lower part of the arm while the lock is applied on the elbow joint.

However, when one analyses judo groundwork, it can be seen that there are many less obvious ways than these of putting the head to good use. It can be used to great effect, for example, when turning the opponent over on to his back for a hold-down. In this case you simply push your head against your opponent's left side while you pull his right arm towards you under his chest with both your hands.

It is also used a great deal for defence purposes on the ground. The body arch, for example, used as a means to throw your opponent over you or to loosen his hold when he is holding you with an immobilization technique, depends for its effect to a great extent on your ability to support the weight of your body on your head and neck.

Against strangulation techniques too, pressing the jaw, chin, sides of the face, etc., against your shoulder, chest, throat, etc., can make it very difficult for your opponent to position his hands in the proximity to your neck, throat, etc., necessary for the application of a strangulation technique. Mr. Kawamura, 7th Dan, when he was in London teaching at the Budokwai, could by moving his head in this manner resist with very little effort even the most determined attempts to apply neck locks on him.

By using the head for the purposes already given, you will gradually increase its usefulness so that you can quite naturally by this training go on to use it in more subtle ways.

32 THIRTY-SECOND PRINCIPLE

Practise the art of tiring your opponent's hands and arms by pulling your jacket suddenly and violently from his grip.

The judo players who have contributed most to this department of skill and knowledge in judo are those who specialize in the throwing technique called Ippon-seoi-nage (One-handed shoulder throw). This is because this technique requires that you hold your opponent's jacket with only one hand in order to initiate the technique, unlike the great majority of the other popular contest-judo techniques which require that in order to initiate them you take a grip on your opponent's jacket with both of your hands.

It can be readily seen therefore why it is to the advantage of a shoulder-throw specialist to prevent his opponent from securing a two-handed grip on his jacket. Because if he can domineer the proceedings so that both of them have only a one-handed grip on each other's jackets, it means that he creates a situation in which he alone can make strong attacks. It is assumed of course that this his opponent does not also specialize in the shoulder-throw.

The sequence of movements which usually occurs if a right-handed ippon-seoi-nage specialist wants a contest to be fought out with each man holding the other's jacket with only one hand is the following. He will first, if you take up a right-handed stance, secure a grip with his left hand on the right side of your jacket usually in between your right lapel and shoulder or lower. This grip will also allow you to take your grip with your right hand on the left side of his jacket in the normal way, but he will then do all in his power to prevent you from taking a hold of his jacket with your left hand. He usually accomplishes this by standing with his left foot forward and his right foot back, which position puts most distance in between your left hand and the right side of his jacket, which of course is the part of the jacket you usually grip with your left hand. This stance alone is usually not enough to prevent a determined judo player from securing a grip with his left hand, so our specialist will also bring his right hand into play by using it to push your left hand away each time it comes near to gripping the right side of his jacket. In this way he will bring about the advantage to himself spoken of in paragraph two. If however, in spite of his precautions with his stance and right-hand work, you manage to secure your left hand grip on the right side of his jacket, he will resort to more violent methods to preserve the advantage which he has worked so hard to get. He will suddenly and violently pull the right side of his jacket out of your grip by dragging the whole right side of his body, from shoulder to hip, back and round to his left. You might succeed in once again getting your left-hand grip. He will simply repeat his previous action and drag his jacket out of your grip again. And he will continue to do this each time you succeed in getting your left hand grip. The effect eventually of this action will be to cause your left hand and arm to tighten up and ache so much that even if you manage to keep your left hand grip for any length of time, you will not be able to use it with much effect.

Of course, with practice against this type of individual, your hand and arm will get used to the strain imposed upon them by the constant dragging of the jacket away from your hand, but there are some judo men who are so practised and strong in this art of forcing their opponents to relinquish their grip by dragging their body in the opposite direction that it is almost impossible to get a grip on them strong enough to allow you to throw them. One such person is Mr. Inokuma, who became Japanese Judo Champion, World Champion, and Olympic Gold Medallist. He specializes in Ippon-seoi-nage and very often will start a contest by grabbing his opponent's right lapel, and not his left which is normal, with his right hand. He has become with the passage of time so expert with this method of holding that it is very difficult indeed even for very experienced judo players to get a proper hold on his jacket. If you try to hold his left lapel, collar, etc., he will prevent this by pushing you with his right hand against your right shoulder and at the same time drag his left shoulder away. This combined action makes it extremely difficult to either take or preserve once you have taken, a right hand hold on his jacket. If on the other hand you try to grip the right side of his jacket with your left hand, he will transfer his right-hand hold on your right lapel, shoulder, etc. to his left hand and drag the right side of his jacket forcefully out of your left hand. He will continue in this manner to spoil your chances of getting a proper grip on his jacket and at the same cause your hands and arms to become very tired, which of course reduces their efficiency as agents of either attack or defence and diminishes greatly your chances of throwing him or of offering much resistance to his shoulder throw.

Now, although the shoulder throw specialists will be able, because of reasons already given, to make the best use of this kind of strategy, there is no reason at all why every judo player should not incorporate it in his repertoire of skills. Because if he does not practise and become skilful and strong in the methods which will enable him to exhaust his opponent's hands and arms, he will be at a very serious disadvantage indeed when he comes up against people like Inokuma. The point to realize is that in a judo contest if you can show your opponent that you are just as skilful in the use of a certain strategism as he is, you can deter him from using it, due to the fact that he will realize that in your particular case he will not be able to achieve the object of a strategism, which of course is to give one an advantage over one's opponent. If, on the other hand, he sees that you are not practised at all in the use of a certain strategism, or that you are practised in its use but not as well practised as he is himself, he will most certainly not be slow to push home his advantage.

The ideal, of course, in the case of the particular strategism which this principle is concerned with, is for you yourself to become so skilful and strong in its use that you will be able not only to deter your opponent from using it, but that you will in fact be able to overpower him with it.

33 THIRTY-THIRD PRINCIPLE

Seek out and practise with strong and heavy people. This is the best way to develop real determination, power, confidence, and a clear appreciation of the necessity of leverage.

What is a tremendous source of satisfaction for a judo player is when he has the confidence in his ability to compete on at least equal terms with an opponent irrespective of the opponent's style, height, strength, or weight.

Only intelligent and careful choice of technique will enable one to do this with regards to the problem of the opponent's style and height. However, when it comes to the problem of competing with opponents who are stronger or heavier or both stronger and heavier than oneself, then the only way to eventually get to be able to compete with them on fairly equal terms is to constantly put the thirty-third principle into practice. There is no short cut, alternative, or easy way out. Of course the use of one's intelligence can do nothing but make the problem easier, but intelligence alone in this case is quite insufficient.

This is so because although it is possible through hard training and the use of one's ingenuity to be able to beat opponents superior to oneself in both strength and weight, the real problem is how to go about handling those who are not only superior to oneself in both strength and weight, but who are also as conscientious as oneself when it comes to hard training and whose common sense and ingenuity are equal to one's own.

The solution to the problem lies in the development of your powers of leverage to their maximum, which means that your movements when applying technique, etc., should stem right from the soles of your feet and not simply from your shoulders or even hips. This of course requires a great deal of practice in order to be able to do it quickly enough so that you do not betray your intentions and allow your opponent to prevent himself from being thrown. And the only way to develop this ability to apply the degree of leverage necessary to throw a person much stronger and heavier than oneself is to take every available opportunity to practise with strong and heavy people, as this ability can only be developed by constantly exposing your body to the degree of resistance which only strong and heavy people can impose upon it.

Another benefit which is gained by practising regularly with people stronger and heavier than oneself and which reduces the natural advantage which they have over one, is that when practising with this kind of partner, one is forced to put to much greater use one's natural assets such as determination, aggression, concentration, etc. As it is only by using these assets to their fullest that one can beat an opponent who is equally as skilful as oneself but who has a weight and strength advantage. And it is this latter benefit which more than any other which can accrue to one by practising with strong and heavy partners which will enable you to drastically reduce the natural advantage already referred to. This is so because the naturally strong and heavy person never gets as much practice as his weaker and lighter brother in developing to their fullest the natural assets already spoken of, due to the fact that these are only really put to the test when one is pitting them against opponents stronger and heavier than oneself, which of course in the case of the strong and heavy person occurs comparatively infrequently.

Finally, although the main object in practising regularly with partners stronger and heavier than oneself is to offset as much as possible the natural advantage which they have over you, your courage will be well rewarded in another important way too. Because it is a well known fact that the more one practises with strong and heavy partners the easier it becomes to defeat people of one's own strength and weight or less.

34 THIRTY-FOURTH PRINCIPLE

In order to disturb a person's balance well enough to throw him powerfully, one must synchronize one's hand action on his jacket with the leverage of one's own body stemming right from the soles of one's feet.

This principle is of such great importance in judo that from the very first time that you start practising throwing technique, you should also start putting this principle into practice. The reason for this is that its correct application requires such great subtlety that unless you develop it as a natural part of your throwing technique right from the outset of your judo training, there is the very great danger that you will never get to be able to apply with the degree of naturalness required in throwing powerfully, experienced or strong and heavy opponents. And unless you can throw this type of opponent, you can never be considered as having developed true expertise, as it is only this kind of expertise which makes it possible. And undoubtedly one of the main ingredients of this kind of expertise is the ability to apply this principle with perfect naturalness. A judo player without this ability is suffering from as great a lack in his judo armoury, as it were, as he is when his timing is at fault, or his technique is inadequate, or his movements are done with insufficient speed, etc.

What this principle means is that when you initiate any judo throwing technique, you do it by disturbing your opponent's balance in such a way that when you commit yourself to those actions which follow this disturbing of your opponent's balance and which constitute the rest of the technique, your chances of completing the technique and throwing your opponent could not possibly be better. And what this involves is that you coordinate your hand action on your opponent's jacket with a levering action of your whole body stemming right from the soles of your feet. This means that your feet should be firmly planted on the ground, so that when you see, make, or sense an opportunity to apply technique, your feet can do their job properly, which is to dig into the ground so that they give your body a very firm base from which to exert an unbalancing effect on your opponent via your hands pulling your opponent's jacket.

Now why this is so difficult to do, and which is the reason why you must start practising it as soon as you take up judo, is that for it to work, you have to co-ordinate the planting of your feet into the mat with the moment the opponent's foot on the side of his body where you will apply your technique is just about to sink into the mat. And this is very difficult to do against experienced judo players because they are constantly watching the maneuvering you may make with your feet and adapt their own to foil your intentions, which is why what in theory seems to be a perfectly simple thing turns out to be one of the most difficult things in judo to do really well consistently. But to do it well must be one of the aims of the ambitious judo player.

Practice accompanied by common sense will eventually enable you to do it with the necessary degree of naturalness required in all judo movement, but what is of major importance, and is in fact the main object of this article, is that judo players should realize how essential to their real progress is the ability to dominate their opponent right at the start of a throwing technique by commencing the destruction of his balance in the manner described, which in judo terminology is called Kuzushi.

Basing your judo training on this realization therefore is the only way to ensure that you achieve whatever judo potential you may possess. On the other hand, if you ignore this very basic principle of judo, Kuzushi, and attempt to substitute for it mere speed of movement and so-called freedom of movement, which is often with good intentions but mistakenly advocated, you may very well progress well enough during the early stages of your judo career, but when the competition gets more experienced, you will fail miserably as an effective judo player. Even if later on you decide that, after all, intelligent and consistent application of Kuzushi is the only way to become really effective in judo, it will require a great deal of time and patience to rid you of your earlier formed and ineffective habits.

35 THIRTY-FIFTH PRINCIPLE

Use judo as a basis for philosophical thought, but do not be so unreasonable as to expect judo to provide you with an insight into the truths of life without first having practised the art for a long period of time.

As the writings of the late Gunji Koizumi, 7th Dan, founder of the famous Budokwai Club and the man mainly responsible for having introduced judo to Britain, show us, judo can be a great basis for philosophical thought. The complexity and depth of Mr. Koizumi's writings on the philosophic side of judo showed very clearly a mind used to struggling with problems which could lend themselves to a man's getting closer and closer to ultimate reality. And during his lifetime, he must have influenced the minds and attitudes of a very large number of people with his philosophical approach to life which came from his judo training. This influence was so great on the judo world of Great Britain that judo and philosophizing became closely related activities for many judo enthusiasts, who would wait impatiently for their next copy of the Budokwai Judo Bulletin, which was Mr. Koizumi's medium for his dissertations on judo philosophy.

At the present time, although judo does not have the same philosophical image which Mr. Koizumi gave to it via his writings, etc., it is still associated in the minds of many people with philosophy. But, unfortunately, there are still a lot of people, as was also the case in Mr. Koizumi's day, who think that as soon as they join a judo club, don a judo suit, and commence to practise basic judo technique, they will immediately be transformed into an habitual searcher of truth. And when they discover after maybe some months of judo training that they are, if they are truthful, as still as reluctant to come to grips intellectually with problems of a philosophical nature as they were when they had no judo training behind them, they become disillusioned with judo as a system of mental culture and decide to give it up. They have usually made the mistake of philosophizing and theorizing instead of training.

Because the fact of the matter is that if judo, or any challenging activity for that matter, is to be used as a basis for philosophical reasoning, one must first of all concentrate one's efforts on mastering the technical part of the activity. Because it is, as any honest philosopher will confirm, only via exposing oneself to and cheerfully or at least willingly accepting the struggle which this attempt at mastery involves, that the philosophical foundations of one's personality are laid. And this simply means that you very, very gradually, by accepting the challenge of this struggle, become increasingly aware of the meaning of the conception referred to as Truth. And with this awareness also comes the realization that worthwhile progress of any kind is only possible by applying the tenacity and magnanimity which the discovery and acceptance of truth require. And this in turn, because of this realization, is where you will gradually strengthen the already developing habit of using your intellect, personality, and experience in a way which will best enable you to build up your fund of truth. And once this happens, it is only a question of time before this habit will enable you to achieve the philosopher's object, the attainment of wisdom.

On the other hand, if you attempt to achieve this object via judo without training with the object in mind of mastering the technical part of the activity and becoming an expert in the true sense of the word, your methods of training will never be of the kind which could ever hope to open for you the doors of truth, as it were. And instead of attaining to wisdom, you will become nothing better than a theorist, with no real ability at all in distinguishing truth from what only appears to be truth.

36 THIRTY-SIXTH PRINCIPLE

Thinking about a contest on the eve of a contest can only result in a diminished chance of your winning it.

One of the greatest enemies of the contest judo player is nerves. And personally I have never known anyone who was not nervous before a judo contest. And although it is claimed by many people that this nervousness is a sign that they are really concerned with winning the contest, and that it gives an edge, sharpness, etc., to their movements, I feel that they are simply making an attempt to justify a condition over which they have no control, and if they were truthful they would much rather prepare for and participate in contests without having to tolerate the sickening effect which nerves has on them.

All this is rather hypothetical, however, as all contest judo players, including Japanese, who perhaps do not show it so much, experience nervous tension when a contest is approaching, on the eve of a contest, and on the day on which the contest is held. But there are things which can help one to reduce, as much as it is possible to do so in one's own particular case, this nervous tension, which if left uncontrolled can play havoc with one's performance.

And as probably the worst time for most people in the case of participating in a judo contest is the eve of the contest, it is this time with which one should be most concerned with regards to the ways and means best calculated to bringing under control nervous tension. And undoubtedly the only way to do it is to avoid at any cost whatsoever any thought or mention of the following day's contest. This, one could easily say, is easier said than done. And it is true that putting into practice this thirty-sixth principle is not by any means easy to do. But with practice, and that is the key to its successful application, it can be done. I personally found that, with practice, I was able eventually to banish disturbing thoughts almost completely from my mind on the eve of the contest and so I would be quite untroubled by the nervous tension that can keep one awake all night long and consequently almost completely ruins one's chances of doing one's best.

The trick is to act in such a way on the eve of a contest that you keep your mind occupied all day with little activities which do not put a strain on you mentally or physically but are such that will keep your mind pleasantly absorbed so that it is distracted from the contest of the following day. If you are engaged in the type of work which is physically or mentally exhausting, it is better to have a day off on the eve of the contest, as it is important to reserve one's energies for the contest and not dissipate them on your job. Most bosses these days are I am sure broad minded enough to give you a day off if they see that the contest means a lot to you. If on the other hand, your job is not exhausting, then it is better to go to work on the eve of the contest. This will enable you to occupy your mind with your work and so keep it off the contest. It will also have the effect of tiring you, not straining you mark you, so that by the time you go to bed later in the evening you will have little trouble in getting to sleep. If you have decided to have a day off, you should make sure too that your activities will also have the effect of tiring you somewhat. And the best way to do this for most people is to have a nice leisurely stroll for about an hour. It is a good idea to do everything in this leisurely fashion on the day before a contest, as this helps to keep the nerves in check. Take your time over your meals for example, have a nice leisurely read of the newspaper, watch television for a while, have a game of cards, billiards, drafts. But whatever you do, make sure that it is done in a leisurely manner, and if you find that whatever you are doing is placing some kind of mental or physical strain on you, do something else. The whole idea is to get through the day without unduly tiring yourself or irritating yourself, but at the same time to keep yourself from thinking about the contest. And if you find that in spite of your precautions your mind occasionally fixes itself on the contest, you must immediately, without any ifs or buts, either fix it on to something else or simply not think of anything at all. You will of course find this difficult to do at first, but with practice it becomes comparatively easy.

The best way to get through the evening is either to go the cinema or to the theatre, depending on your taste, but try to avoid seeing the kind of film or play that will remind you of the following day's contest. A good type of film or play if available is a good comedy, which will not only keep your mind off the contest quite effectively, but will also brighten your mood in case you are feeling a bit tense or miserable.

By the time you return home after your evening's entertainment, which should not be too late of course as you should try to get to bed around ten or eleven, you should be tired just enough to enable you to go to bed and get to sleep without too much difficulty, you will find too that having rid your mind all day of any thoughts of the contest each time they came to you, you will because of this habit most likely be undisturbed by any such thoughts while in bed. But if you are, this habit will also enable you to banish them quite effectively, resulting in your getting to sleep and sleeping soundly in preparation for the contest the next day.

37 THIRTY-SEVENTH PRINCIPLE

Practise Kata occasionally because Kata does embody many useful judo principles, but never substitute Kata practice for the far, far more essential Randori (Free Practice).

In judo, due to the inherent difficulty of its techniques, it is absolutely essential for the judo enthusiast to choose a method of training which will enable him to attain to at least a certain degree of mastery of these techniques in the shortest time possible. If he does not do this, the chances are that he will get little satisfaction from his judo activity and consequently give it up. And it is this little simple fact which teachers must be very much aware of when arranging training schedules, syllabuses for examinations, etc. It is the old story of success breeding success.

Now, the fact of the matter is that although traditionally Kata training is a part of a judo player's activities, it is not the kind of training which one should do very much of in the early stages of one's judo career. This is because it cannot be reconciled with the truth expressed in the previous paragraph. The best time, for the vast majority of people who do judo to start learning kata is after they have become hooked on judo, as it were, and know that it will take a great deal for them even to think about giving it up. If they do this, they will be able to devote all of their attentions to the kind of training which is more designed than any other kind to developing mastery of judo technique in the most satisfying way. This training is called randori (Free Practice), which if done properly and regularly enables one in a comparatively short time to experience the satisfaction and thrills which come from being able to throw one's opponent, control him with groundwork technique, and also to be able to resist his attempts to throw or control with groundwork technique oneself. And once a person begins to experience judo in this way, his training sessions become for him more meaningful, and he is therefore able to not only put more into these sessions, he also finds that he can train for much longer periods of time, which of course is the only way in the case of judo to gain mastery over its technique.

At what point in one's judo career therefore should one begin to take an interest in judo kata. This of course is not an arbitrary part of one's judo training, as it is probably necessary according to one's judo association grading examination syllabus to be able to perform some kata in order to pass the theoretical part of grading examinations for Black Belt promotions. One must therefore start preparing for these examinations after reaching the grade of 1st kyu (Brown Belt) which of course is the grade before Sho-dan (First Grade Black Belt).

And it is this stage which is for most judo enthusiasts the most crucial, because this is when they have to really start getting down to hard, regular, training based on intelligent methods, if they are to compete successfully with the opposition which gets tougher and tougher the higher they get up the grading ladder. And unless one at this point develops the habit of hard training to the point where it is possible to do this kind of hard training without experiencing undue physical strain and nervous tension each time one has a training session, one will find it very difficult to do the amount of randori and uchi-komi training necessary to one's having a chance of defeating the opposition in high grade contests. In other words, one can quite easily at this point, due to the fact that one has no alternative but to practise kata in order to pass the theoretical part of examinations for promotion to Dan grade, become someone who is good at performing kata but not much good at defeating opponents in contest. And of course this is the old but unfortunately quite common mistake of putting the cart before the horse, because the simple fact is that to gain any real benefit from the practice of kata one must be trained via the practice of randori and uchikomi to a pitch where one's body can easily apply the subtle principles which the kata embodies. If on the other hand, one's body is not trained to this pitch, then one can never in quite a natural manner put into practice the kata principles against a strong opponent, which of course makes kata training in this case a waste of time. It is therefore not a question of doing kata training for its own sake but in order to become aware of the principles which are embodied in kata, which if applied when we do our randori training will enable us better to make effective our techniques.

This object or aim of kata training, if clearly grasped, will enable you not only to derive the greatest possible benefit from this training, but will help you to avoid the very great danger of using kata training as an alternative method of training to Randori, which, as we have seen, it is not meant to be.

38 THIRTY-EIGHTH PRINCIPLE

Make it a Golden Rule to look for and practise with Left-Handers.

In Judo the natural left-hander has a distinct advantage over his right-handed opponents. That this is so can be proved by a little simple mathematical effort. Supposing, for example, that in a judo club there are forty members. The odds are that not more than two of these will be natural left-handers. Now, let us suppose that the practice is evenly distributed, as it were. That is that everybody in the club practises with everybody else. And this of course, more or less, is what does actually happen at judo clubs. The left-handers will, therefore, out of thirty-nine sessions of free practice (Randori), practise with thirty-eight right-handers and one left hander. The right-handers, however, will practise with only two left-handers, and the rest of the thirty-seven people with whom they practise will be, like themselves, right-handers. It can be easily seen, therefore, that the left-hander, because of the large number of times he practises with right-handers, has a very good chance of building up a strong defence against right-handed technique, which is of course the technique which right-handers specialize in. The right-hander, however, because of the small number of times he practises with left-handers, does not have a good chance at all of building up a strong defence against left-handed technique, which of course is the technique which left-handers specialize in.

The advantage which the left-hander has, therefore, is nothing to do with his having more natural skill, power, etc., than a right-hander, because of course he does not. It is simply because he has a much greater chance of getting used to what his right-handed opponents do than they have of getting used to what he does. In fact, if we take the figures used in the previous paragraph as being average, which they are, we can see that the left-hander has more chance of getting used to right-handers than the right-hander has of getting used to left handers. And, obviously, as defence plays a very important role in judo, this constitutes for the left-hander a great advantage.

This fact has been recognized by judo players for a long time, but until it is shown mathematically just why this is so, it is difficult to see how great this advantage is. Once realized however, it is a tremendous incentive to do something about it. And the only constructive thing one can do about it is to put this, the THIRTY-EIGHTH PRINCIPLE, into practice.

Where, one may ask, is one to find the left-handed opposition, however? We have already seen that they are few and far between. The fact of the matter is that because most people steer clear of natural left-handers as though they were the carriers of some deadly contagious disease, it is quite an easy thing to ignore the few left-handers in one's club. Very often, if they are good and also big and heavy as well as being natural left-handers, they can most likely be found in some corner of the dojo impatiently waiting for some hero to ask them for a practice. And the fact is that unless you have put this present principle into practice conscientiously for quite a lengthy period of time, it does require courage to take the initiative required to request them to practise with you instead of waiting for them to ask you to practise with them. Because it does require a lot of practice with natural left-handers before you can prevent them from consistently throwing you about. But with time, you will find that unlike the people who stay clear of good left-handers in training sessions and who never give themselves a real chance to get used to them, you will when you meet left-handers in contest be able to give a good account of yourself.

39 THIRTY-NINTH PRINCIPLE

Respect the Grading System and the Status of those Judoists who by long personal, practical experience have qualified as Dan-Grade Holders (Black-Belt Holders).

This principle is concerned with the claim being made today that simply because a person has a Black-Belt Grade he is not necessarily a good teacher, and that therefore to become a teacher of judo, it is not necessary to make the kind of effort necessary to being graded to Black Belt.

Well of course the first part of the argument is correct, because the kind of activity one has to engage in in order to develop the skill, power, etc., which are necessary to obtain a Black-Belt Grade, is concerned with only one's own judo education. Which concern, being in a sense selfish, is quite different to the concern for others, which is the chief motivating force of the successful teacher.

The latter half of the argument however that claims "that therefore to become a good teacher of judo it is not necessary to make the kind of effort necessary to being graded to Black Belt" is not really indicative of a logical train of thought. Because although this concern for others which very good teachers have is important to a teacher, it in itself is not sufficient. A teacher must also have a personal, practical experience of the subject which he teaches. If he does not possess this kind of experience, the very admirable concern for others which he may have will be largely wasted via teaching this subject. He is in the same situation as the very good but poor man who would give you the shirt from off his back, but who unfortunately because of his own impoverished condition cannot even afford to wear one himself.

In judo, the practical, personal experience which a teacher needs in order to do a good job of teaching others is gained in only one way, and that is to expose oneself to the training which one has to do in order to become a Dan Grade. The skill and knowledge which this experience provides one with will not, however, enable one immediately to teach well, because, as we have seen in the first and second paragraph of this article, one's attitude to the job of teaching is of great importance and one may not possess to any marked extent any of the virtues which seem to be the hallmark of a good teacher. It is often said that good teachers are born, not made. Be this as it may, assuming that one has exerted oneself to the extent that one has been graded to Dan Grade, one will, given the opportunity to teach regularly that is, develop into a competent enough teacher of judo.

However, if one can combine one's practical, personal experience as a player who has reached Dan-Grade standard, with what is best described as a good teaching attitude, which some people have as a natural gift and which others can develop given time to adapt their personalities to teaching, one does if one teaches regularly become the best possible kind of teacher. And there is no doubt, although there are some exceptional people who are fairly good judo teachers even though they have not reached Dan-Grade standard, that in order to become this best possible kind of teacher, one has no alternative but to make the effort required to become a Black-Belt in a Judo Association with a good standard of grading. There is no other way to do it. Some of the Dan-Grade Holders, among others of course, who epitomize this best possible kind of teacher are T. P. Leggett, Syd Hoare, Dickie Bowen, Malcolm Hopkinson, and Tony Reay, who over the years have done such an excellent job of teaching judo and producing first-class judo men at the famous Budokwai Club in London.

40 FORTIETH PRINCIPLE

By far the best way to learn judo is to watch and practise with High-Grade judo men, and then attempt to copy the way in which these High-Grades do their techniques, especially their favourite techniques.

This principle assumes that the club at which you practise judo has among its members High-Grade judo men. And these days, unless you live in a village or very small town, you should have at least two or three High-Grade judo men at your club.

And in this respect the judo enthusiast of to-day is very fortunate compared with the judo enthusiast of only a few years ago, when in order to put into practice this principle regularly, he was very often forced to travel long distances to clubs where High-Grades practised, or the club where he was a member but which had no High-Grades practising there would have to arrange for a visiting High-Grade to do a week-end's course. And as these week-end courses were arranged only very occasionally and only by the more conscientious clubs, and furthermore were for the most part devoted to instruction and not actual randori, the judo players who attended these courses did not get much of an opportunity to put this principle into practice.

When I first started doing judo, which was at The Newcastle Judo Club, Newcastle Upon Tyne, I had the good fortune of having High-Grade judo men like the chief instructors George Bamford and Les Crowe and the star pupil Billy Litely practising there. And this of course made a great difference to the speed with which I was able to make progress, as I could put this principle into practise. But as a provincial judo club, The Newcastle Judo Club was quite exceptional, as most provincial judo clubs had no High-Grades at all.

But it was not until Pat Mohan and I decided to pack our bags and leave Newcastle Upon Tyne for London where we started doing judo at the famous Budokwai that I realized how much I had to be thankful for to Mr. George Bamford, Mr. Les Crowe, and Mr. Billy Litley for the opportunity they had given me to practise with and watch High-Grades in action. Because I soon realized that other judo players who came from the provinces to the Budokwai were, compared with Pat Mohan and myself, very weak indeed, and had very little knowledge of fighting judo techniques.

The Budokwai of course was a wonderful place for a young judo enthusiast to practise with and watch numerous High-Grade judo-ka in action, and it had an atmosphere more conducive to the practising of a serious activity like judo than almost any other dojo I have ever been to, including Japan. And so, over the years, until I left England, I practised with and took every opportunity to watch the High-Grade Black Belts of the Budokwai in action.

I did this so much that I can even to-day still remember in detail the different techniques, styles, and idiosyncrasies of every judo player who ever wore a Black Belt at the Budokwai at that time: Mr. Koizumi's famous hip movement for example; T. P. Leggett's very live style and also his right O-uchi-gari throw; Percy Sekine's fighting spirit and Seoi-otoshi when he competed at the Albert Hall with Mr. Daigo, Japanese Judo Champion; Charlie Grant's neck locks; Ian Morris's left Tai-otoshi to the side holding the tip of the sleeve; Geoff Gleeson's left O-uchi-gari/left Tai-otoshi combination and his high left-hand grip; Charlie Palmer's right De-ashi-barai and Counter Techniques (Charlie is now president of the International Judo Federation as well as being Chairman of the British Judo Association); Dickie Bowen's left Ippon-seoi-nage and Ko-uchi-gari combination and also his counter technique which he used with such good effect in the first World Judo Championships in Tokyo; the devastating right Hane-goshi of Dennis Bloss; the equally devastating left Uchi-mata of Doug Young; the power-house movement of Alfie Grahber when going through a line-up with his right Tai-otoshi; the very excellent technique of the left-hander Don Burr, now in Australia. A great loss to British judo; the classical grace and effectiveness of Reg Whiteford's judo; Dennis Robertson's dynamic movement and spinning-in techniques; Warwick P. Steptoe's great expertise with feints using both left and right throwing techniques; the extremely effective and aesthetic Uchi-mata on the right of George Whyman which stood him in great stead when he later went to Japan; Zipeure's right-hand swinging action when he did his very scientific Morote-seoi-nage; the notorious Pete Foster arm locks which would have put to shame many Aikido experts; the powerful groundwork techniques of the ex-wrestler Don Burgess; the Ko-soto-gari and expertise on the ground of Tony Harrington; the almost miraculous left Harai-goshi technique of Ralph Smith (he had two fingers missing from his left hand); Chaplain's uncanny sense of timing with his left Ippon-seoi-nage and Sode-tsurikomi-goshi; the New Zealander Havecan and his irresistible right O-soto-guruma and Ashi-waza; the dreaded Tam McDermott from Glasgee who in spite of a ninety per cent disability condition when he left the army became via his very skilful judo (right Harai-goshi and left Tsuri-komi-goshi) one of the best judo men in Britain; Rab Smith, professional colleague of Tam, from Edinburgh and now living in Australia, who was undoubtedly, with the exception of one man, the hardest worker I knew, and who had the most powerful Morote-seoi-nage and Okuri-ashi-barai I ever came across until I went to Japan; the other member of the Scottish contingent at that time, then referred to by McDermott and company as Wee Kerr as he was very young, was George Kerr, with whom I trained in Japan some time later. He was trying right and left technique at the time but later settled for only left technique, thus enabling him to become a famous British international, and also middle weight champion of Britain; another Budokwai player at that time was Ben Reed with whom I also trained with in the Kenshusei (special student's section at the Kodokan in Tokyo). He was the living proof of the judo belief that the small man can beat the big man, which he did consistently; John Cornish was also another Budokwai man at that time with whom I was later to train with in Japan, both in Judo and Aikido. John is now National Coach of the British Aikido Association and also chief instructor in this art at the Budokwai.

Thanks to these hard-working and talented judo men, and others too numerous to mention, I was given the opportunity to apply consistently over a period of years this fortieth principle. Which experience when I went to Japan was of untold benefit to me, as I found that I had developed the powers of observation and courage and the ability to copy which applying this principle correctly involves. And by constantly applying it over the seven years of my judo training in Japan I gave myself the best possible chance to derive the greatest possible benefit from my stay there.

Of course, it must not be thought that any one person has either the time, energy, or talent to be able to develop expertise with all of the many judo techniques which one sees judo experts specializing in; one must be content with developing those techniques which are suitable for oneself. But the powers of observation which applying this principle can develop help one immensely in studying the technique and strategy of those judo players whom you may have to meet in contest, which is a very important part of one's judo training.

Finally, when teaching judo, it is not enough simply to depend for one's teaching material on only that skill which one has been able to develop oneself. Because this will, when compared with the vast amount of skill contained in the whole of judo, be extremely limited. One must therefore be able to teach also those skills which one may not be particularly proficient in oneself. And undoubtedly the best way to develop a vast repertoire of material for the purpose of teaching pupils constructive and realistic judo, apart from some of the merely theoretical instruction which some teachers due to their lack of real knowledge use, is to put into practice the fortieth principle so consistently that its application becomes a natural part of your whole judo plan.

41 FORTY-FIRST PRINCIPLE

Never do Randori (Free Practice) or Shiai (Contest) when the body is cold and stiff; always warm up.

One of the main causes of injury in judo is the fact that judo players very often fail to warm up the body before starting to do randori. Some beginners to judo contest even fail to warm up before engaging in contest. However, in the case of randori, this type of foolishness is certainly not limited to beginners. And when one realizes just what havoc injury in judo can play with one's progress and one's enthusiasm, it is very difficult to understand the attitude of judoists who time and time again neglect to warm up the body with warming-up exercises before engaging in free practice.

The problem of course is one of disinclination; disinclination to do certain exercises for a period of five minutes or so, which for some people is boring, especially when compared to the more exciting and satisfying activity of free practice. And there is no doubt that even the most conscientious of judo players are frequently assailed by this disinclination to go through the process of warming the body up with exercises before commencing randori.

How then do we handle this problem which if left unsolved can and of course often does result in a person's having to stop doing judo altogether due to injury. There is only one way to handle this problem of disinclination no matter in what part of your judo training it may occur. And this way is simply to develop habits which become so strong that in the face of them disinclination wilts. In the case of disinclination to warm up properly before practising randori, you must develop the habit of going through a certain set of exercises before doing randori.

Well of course, as is the case with developing many habits, at first one will be tempted not to do it too conscientiously. Now the best way to make the process of warming up easy for yourself is to go through the same set of exercises in exactly the same sequence each time that you warm up before randori. The reason why this is the best way is because after having done it a few times, there is no reason for you to have to put yourself to the trouble of having to think up something new, which effort one does not always feel like making just before commencing to practise randori, and which can make you skip your warming up. Doing the same exercises in exactly the same sequence will in other words become for you quite quickly a very mechanical thing. And the fact of the matter is that when trying to develop a habit, which in this case is of course the habit of warming up before randori, the more mechanical your actions become, the easier it is for the habit to develop.

And once having developed the habit of warming up before commencing free practice, you will find too that it is much easier to get along to the club to do your judo training, because you will know that the habit is so strong that there will be no danger of your skipping your warming up and consequently risking injury during randori.

Another valuable attribute of habitually doing warming-up exercises before randori is that gradually the effect of the exercises, although primarily to stretch and heat the different parts of the body so as to prevent tearing, overstretching, etc., of these parts, is to give added strength and suppleness to your muscles, joints, tendons, and ligaments, which strength and suppleness are of great value to the judo player.

However, let it not be forgotten that the main reason for warming up before engaging in the violent activity of randori is to avoid injury while thus engaged. And undoubtedly anything which helps one to avoid injury in judo to the extent that warming up does is worthy of the title of principle.

42 FORTY-SECOND PRINCIPLE

If you have an injury, no matter how slight, never run the risk of aggravating it by doing randori (free practice). Whether you apply the same caution in the case of a contest will be determined by how much importance you place on winning the contest. As a general rule, however, concern for the injured part should override all other considerations.

There is only one way to develop judo ability. And that is to practise. And of course the more you practise, the faster and the more satisfactory is your progress. If for example you practise two or three times per week for about an hour and a half each time, you can over a period of one year make very good progress indeed. I am assuming of course that the place or club where you train has competent instructors, who can guide you as to the best techniques for you personally to practise, the best type of grip to specialize in, the best way to do the techniques which you have been told to practise, etc. And of course there must also be enough members of your club enthusiastic enough about judo to enable you to get a reasonable variety of opponents to practise with.

Given these things, you will, after one year's judo training without interruption, be a vastly different individual from the point of view of judo ability to what you were a year before. You will, as it were, find yourself riding on the wave of success. However, as success breeds success, the tendency is for many judo players at this stage to become greedy for progress, to a point where they throw all caution to the wind in an attempt to develop as quickly as possible the power which they are beginning more and more to feel within themselves.

What happens is that they find that the regular practising of the technique or techniques which they specialize in enables them to move their bodies and throw and handle their opponents with a lot of power. And it is, ironically as it may seem, at this point that, unless you are extra careful when practising, you become prey much more to injury than before you develop judo power. Because at this point you begin to start using the natural movement which specialization develops, and which enables you, unlike the movement of an untrained person, to act with a lot of power without thinking. This, coupled with the fact that in order to test your power you make it a point to practise with people as powerful as yourself, can unfortunately result in your occasionally sustaining some kind of injury.

The wisest thing of course when you feel yourself developing power to the point where it is very difficult to exert control over it, is to practise in a reasonably cautious manner and not hurl yourself about in an unthinking manner until you have got a lot more experience in handling this power. This is the best way to avoid getting injured.

This advice is however not too easy to follow, especially if you are very keen and fit. If, therefore, you find that you cannot follow it consistently, and find that you are getting the knocks and bruises which are only a natural consequence of ignoring it, you must if you wish to continue practising judo for any length of time, adopt the following plan.

When you get an injury, even a slight one, which fortunately most judo injuries are, make it a point never to do anything which may cause it to be aggravated. Because, and this will be confirmed by any sportsman, the worst possible kind of injury is an aggravated one. Not because they are more painful, although of course this is often the case as well, but because they take a long time to clear up. In fact the main cause of a chronic injury is allowing an original injury to become aggravated by hurting the same spot again and again before the injured part has had a chance to recover completely.

Due to the length of time that aggravated injuries take in clearing up, therefore, they militate against what we have already seen is the only way to make worthwhile judo progress, which is regular uninterrupted practice. Of course one could argue that if one stops practising randori each time one sustains some slight injury, then this too interrupts one's practice. And of course this is the argument used by those who foolishly advocate wrapping the injured part up and continuing to practise. The answer is that it is almost inevitable that occasionally one will get some slight injury; a twisted big toe or a pulled muscle for example. So therefore one must accept the fact that when this happens, it is far wiser to use a little patience and stop doing free practice for the short period of time necessary for these slight injuries to clear up completely than to carry on practising and running the very real risk of injuring the same part again before it has had a chance to heal, and finding that you have an aggravated injury on your hands, which as we have already seen can force you to stop practising for a long period of time.

So we are faced with the choice of either accepting the almost inevitable in judo, the slight injury, and giving up practising for a fairly short period of time till it gets better, despite the fact that it does of course, but only to a minor extent, militate against the rule of uninterrupted practice as the only way to make worthwhile progress in judo. Or, by carrying on doing randori when we have an injury so that we do not interrupt our training, risking hurting the same spot again and perhaps again and finally having to admit that we have an aggravated injury and must therefore interrupt our training for perhaps quite a long time so as to give the injury time to heal.

The way to look at this question so that we can have confidence in our choice is to realize that sustaining an aggravated injury is not in the least inevitable, is only developed by misdirected enthusiasm, and therefore should never be the cause of our having to interrupt our training for a long period of time. Whereas the slight injury is, fortunately not frequently, almost inevitable. Which is why we are perfectly justified in interrupting our training for the short period of time these slight injuries take to heal, without feeling in the slightest guilty about having to make this interruption in our randori training.

43 FORTY-THIRD PRINCIPLE

Use Judo as a means of developing Courage.

Being a Martial Art, one of the functions of judo is to enable those who practise it to become proficient in Self Defence. It is therefore essential that the kind of judo training that you do enables you to develop courage, because without courage, it is quite difficult to do real justice to your skill with judo technique as a good means of self-defence. If, for example, you were attacked by a gang of hoodlums, which is not an uncommon occurrence these days, which can often mean that you have to literally fight for your life, you would fare very badly indeed unless you could execute your judo technique in a very aggressive manner. And when I say aggressive I do not mean the comparatively ineffectual aggression which very often can be engendered by fear. What I am referring to is the confident fearless aggression which can only be engendered by courage.

And this of course is the main reason why in judo you have contests, both grading and championship, because without a doubt, participation in the very-often nerve racking, aggressive, highly competitive judo contest is the very best way to use judo as a means of developing courage. This is so because the nature of a contest is such that unless you learn to act with confidence and fighting spirit in the face of nervous tension or fear, which is what courage is, you have very little chance of beating an opponent who can act like this. And because most people anyway like to win contests, you soon see the necessity of taking a grip of yourself and acting with courage, which means that you have to learn how to conquer fear, which element is inherent in all of us.

Now although participation in contest is the best way via judo training to practise exposing yourself to a situation which engenders fear and then attempting to do what you must do in spite of the fear, which is to act with courage, it is not the only way to practise this. In fact, judo training is replete with opportunities for practising developing courage. The very act of taking up judo is for many people an act of courage in itself. And of course the early weeks and months of your judo training until you begin to develop skill and power constantly demand that you act with courage. But, strangely enough, it is just when they are getting power and skill and have got into the habit of acting in a courageous fashion that many people commence to destroy this solid foundation which has taken them some time and a lot of hard work to lay.

The rot sets in, as it were, from the point of view of judo being for them a medium which will enable them to develop courage, when they realize that they have reached a stage of judo skill and power which enables them to practise with those who are less experienced than themselves and dominate them. In other words they find that there are many people at their club who could not possibly hope to throw them, counter-throw them, or defeat them in groundwork, but who themselves on the other hand can easily be thrown, counter-thrown, and easily handled in groundwork. These people, as it were, are easy meat. And therefore once having grasped the significance of this, they make it a point to practise only with these people, who, because they are unable to present any sort of challenge at all to them, make very little call on their courage. Which of course can be a very pleasant activity. But so is having a pint of beer near the fire in the saloon bar on a cold winter's night. In other words, this kind of training cannot in the least be reconciled with the kind of attitude expected of a person who is supposed to be an exponent of the Martial Art of Judo. And if continued with, you will never develop the courage required to do either very well in judo contests or to ever use judo really effectively as a form of self-defence.

The following simple rules if followed conscientiously will enable you to make the most of your judo training both from the point of view of technical progress and the development of courage. 1. Make it a rule to take the initiative and request others for a practice; do not wait for people to ask you. This develops courage. 2. Try as much as it is possible at your club to do so to practise only with those people who are at least as good as yourself. This also develops courage. 3. Another excellent way to develop courage is never to refuse to practise with anyone no matter how much better he is than yourself, unless your having an injury or some other serious consideration would render it injudicious. 4. Finally, do not stop a practice in order to rest simply because you feel a little tired or winded. Fighting this inclination is probably one of the best ways in judo to develop the will power and determination which are an integral part of real courage.

44 FORTY-FOURTH PRINCIPLE

When doing Randori (free practice) or Uchi-komi (technique repetition practice with a partner), try to avoid being too tensed up.

What is characteristic of a perfectly executed judo technique is the almost magical degree of co-ordination displayed by the person executing it. And if you aspire to real expertise in judo, the expertise that is which enables one to handle even very heavy, strong, experienced judo men with comparative ease, it is absolutely necessary to do everything in your power to acquire this kind of co-ordination.

The main most obvious pre-requisites to having a chance to acquire co-ordination of this magical kind are that you do judo training frequently and regularly with competent training partners, and that you spend most of this training time in specializing in technique, methods of gripping, etc., which are suitable for your particular kind of physique. Everything else is secondary to these two main pre-requisites in your attempt to gain perfect co-ordination not only of the different parts of the body, and the different physical actions, involved in a judo technique, but also of the mental actions which are required in a judo technique.

However, so that you can get the greatest benefit possible from putting into practice these main pre-requisites, it is considered wise by the vast majority of judo teachers in Japan to practise judo, whether it be randori or uchi-komi, without allowing yourself to be tensed up all of the time. It is thought that tension of this kind is destructive to the acquisition of perfect co-ordination, without which, as we have already seen, real expertise is unattainable.

This advice, however, seeming as it does to be almost the antithesis of what one would be expected to do in such an aggressive activity as a martial art like judo, is not that easy to appreciate and follow. So much so that many people never really succeed in following it at all. At the other extreme, some people misconstrue this advice so much that when practising they take on an almost somnambulistic appearance.

What this advice really means is that when practising judo technique, the body and the mind should be kept in a state in between that where they are so tense that complete freedom of movement is difficult and that where they are so relaxed and limp that complete control is lost. In other words, one should try to attain to a happy medium between these two extremes.

For beginners and people without much experience, due to their fear or dislike of being thrown, etc., their poor balance, lack of natural movement, etc., attaining to this happy medium, however, is not an easy thing, and the state in which they practise is usually one of over-tension. And this is particularly apparent when they do free practice with a partner, where the intentions of each is unknown to the other.

It is, however, not nearly as apparent when they do uchi-komi training, where one person stands in a certain position while the other practises the repetition of a certain technique, or techniques, on him without actually going through with the technique and completing the throw. Uchi-komi can therefore be used to great advantage for the purpose of practising your technique without too much mental and physical tension, which state you will gradually also be able to introduce into your randori training.

Attaining to the state where you can practise judo freed from inhibitive mental and physical tension requires time and not a little patience, but the reward of perfect co-ordination and very real judo power which results from practising in this way is one that will compensate you for your efforts a thousand times over.

45 FORTY-FIFTH PRINCIPLE

Never make excuses when beaten in a contest. Be a Good-Loser, and this not just outwardly. Remember that the ultimate object of judo training is to develop in you the magnanimity of the philosopher who never denies the truth. And this is what being a Good-Loser actually implies.

The main reason for not making excuses when beaten in a contest is that it is most unfair to your opponent and therefore contrary to the ethics of sportsman-like behaviour.

The other reason for not making excuses when beaten in a contest is that it tends to become habitual, and once this happens it can have a ruinous effect on your development as a contest judo player.

Why this happens is because your development as a contest judo player depends on one simple, irrefutable fact. This fact is that in order to become a successful contest judo player, that is one who can win contests consistently and not just occasionally, it is imperative that you adopt a very positive attitude towards participation in these contests. In other words, to be able to win contest after contest again and again, you must have at the forefront of your mind each time you fight, one object, and one object only. And this object is to win the contest at any cost, within the rules, of course, which govern judo contests. And the fact of the matter is that the comfort one gets from habitually making excuses when beaten in a contest can persuade you to entertain at the back of your mind the idea of defeat when engaging in one. And this negative idea can only detract from the firmness of your resolution to win at all costs, which as we have seen is the only way to win contests consistently.

Why then do people make excuses when beaten in a contest if it can diminish their chances of doing well as contest men? Obviously, they do not realize that this is true, and instead of eradicating the cause of their need to make excuses, they carry on doing it so that they can save face when defeated in contest. What is this cause which, if you make excuses in this manner, you should eradicate once having realized just what harmful effects this habit of making excuses can have on your contest effectiveness? It is simply any negative notion which can detract from your confidence and your determination to beat your opponent. Because these negative notions, such as lack of confidence in your technique or stamina due to insufficient training as the result of laziness; merely hoping to win instead of knowing that you have no alternative but to win; etc.; are the things you latch on to, as it were, when thinking up a suitable excuse. Eradicate these negative notions, adopt a confident, positive attitude towards contest judo, and you cure yourself of the curse of excuse-making.

You will then, once having destroyed this vicious circle, go on towards true development as a contest judo player. And on those comparatively rare occasions when you are beaten in a contest, knowing that you have done everything in your power to win and therefore feeling no shame because of your defeat, you will feel no need whatsoever to depend on making excuses. You will, in other words, have developed into a true contest judo man, which is to be not only a consistent winner but also to have the magnanimity of a Good-Loser.

46 FORTY-SIXTH PRINCIPLE

Spend some part of your groundwork training in letting your opponent secure a complete hold-down and then practising escaping from it. Inability to escape from hold-downs, due to ignoring this kind of practice, frequently results in the better man being beaten in contest.

What this principle is really directed at are those judo players who are so strong in Tachiwaza (standing judo technique) that they are rarely thrown to the ground and immobilized there with some hold-down technique. And because of this strength in Tachiwaza, they very often tend to neglect to a large extent one of the main aspects of groundwork training, and that is practising in escaping from groundwork techniques.

Of course, their offensive technique in groundwork develops quite naturally, due to the fact that as they are strong in throwing technique, all they have to do to practise offensive groundwork technique is, after throwing their opponent, simply to follow him to the ground and apply some groundwork technique. But as soon as they feel that their opponent is escaping from their technique and might start applying some offensive technique himself, they make it a rule to forsake the groundwork for Tachiwaza and get to their feet, in which position from the point of view of defence they feel much more at home than on the ground.

Well, of course, in contest this is perfectly intelligent strategy, as if one thinks that one is stronger in Tachiwaza than one's opponent, then when engaging in groundwork in which he may be as strong as or stronger than oneself, it is wise, unless one has secured some advantage over him, to get to one's feet as quickly as possible so that one may push home the advantage which one's superiority in Tachiwaza gives one over him. However, even in the case of our very strong judo player practised in all of the wiles and strategisms of contest judo, he will find, comparatively rarely though it may be, that his opponent will manage to apply a hold-down technique on him. And unless he has, as part of his training in groundwork Randori (free practice with opponent), got used to escaping from hold-downs when fully and securely applied, he will have very little chance of escaping from the hold-down in the thirty seconds in which one has to do so, and will as a result lose the contest.

You should, therefore, when doing Randori, not forsake doing groundwork in order to get to your feet each time that you feel that your partner has a chance to start securing a hold-down on you. Instead, let him secure the hold-down and try your hardest to free yourself from it. If you train in this fashion, you will find that you will develop the skill and strength necessary to escape from immobilization techniques, and consequently on those occasions when trapped in this manner by your opponent in a contest, you will have a good chance of freeing yourself.

On the other hand, if you allow disinclination or pride to prevent you from putting this principle into practice when doing Randori, you will have only yourself to blame when beaten in contest with a hold-down by someone who could quite easily be in most respects inferior to you as a judo man.

47 FORTY-SEVENTH PRINCIPLE

Develop your technique so that you have a good chance of defeating your opponent no matter how awkward his stance or posture may be. This of course requires a great deal of thought and practice but is the hallmark of the real expert.

What this principle does not mean is to attempt to use a different throwing technique for each little variation in stance which you meet up with in your opponents. Because if you attempt to do this, ideal though it may appear to be according to some very pure theories, you will have to do so many different techniques that you will never develop the natural movement and power which only comes to you by limiting the number of techniques which you practise. In other words, in order to become an effective judo player, it is quite necessary to specialize in a very small number of throwing techniques. Inokuma, the great Japanese judo champion, and world champion, used to defeat his opponents in contest with almost no other technique but ippon-seoi-nage (one-handed shoulder throw. Anton Geesink, the famous Dutch judo expert, for many years, beat all and sundry with hardly any other throw except uchi-mata (inside thigh throw). Ray Ross, British light heavy weight judo champion who trained at the famous judo university of Tenri in Japan, relies in contest almost entirely on hidari-harai-goshi-makikomi (left outer winding sweeping loin throw). Tony Reay, ex manager of the famous Budokwai Club and now Secretary of the British Judo Association who also trained for a number of years in Japan, epitomizes the principle of specialization with the expertise with which he executes his morote-seoi-nage (two-handed shoulder throw). Another Budokwai personality and good friend of mine with whom for many years I trained in Japan, Malcolm Hopkinson, also shows us with his right harai-makikomi throw the great results to be gained from specialization.

These and many other well known judo men, proving the effectiveness of specialization as they do, show us the folly of splitting our interests too much when it comes to developing effective judo throwing technique. What then do we mean by this forty-seventh principle?

What is meant is that you should, as far as your capacity for specialization permits, specialize in your choice of technique, to the point where you know just what stances and positions taken up by your opponent lend themselves to your throwing him with it, and what stances and positions taken up by your opponent make it almost impossible for you to throw him with your speciality. This is the first essential. This does not mean that you put into the latter category those stances and positions which enable the opponent to offer some resistance to your throw. For example, it would be foolish to be deterred from attempting to use tomoe-nage (stomach throw) simply because your opponent is standing very straight and not bent forward in what is considered to be the ideal position if you want to throw him with tomoe-nage. Because the skill and power which you develop via specialization should enable you to throw your opponent with your favourite technique even if he is not in what is considered to be the ideal position for you to do this. And if you specialize, you will soon see the truth of this, and you will also gradually begin to recognize those stances of your opponents which do present real problems from the point of view of throwing them with your speciality.

What you must do when you come up against these positions which your experience tells you are problematical, is first to try, in your randori training, to find a solution to the problem by sticking as close to your speciality as possible when attempting to throw your opponent who has taken up this difficult position. In other words, you simply adapt your usual method of executing your speciality to your opponent's posture by making any changes to your technique that will enable you better to use it for the purpose of throwing him.

For example, if you specialize in tsuri-komi-goshi and you come up against a person who bends forward and who is not much taller than yourself, you will have to, instead of pushing up strongly with your right hand as you do against an upright stance, pull forward a lot more with this hand at the beginning of the throw, and once having turned your back on your opponent, push forward a lot more with this hand. This use of the right hand is preferable, in the case of this bent forward posture on the part of your opponent if he is not much taller than yourself, to the normal pushing up action which the right hand does when the opponent is upright, because the bent forward posture enables the opponent to resist much more strongly a force attempting to push him upwards than attempting to unbalance him forwards. Of course you should always try to impose as much upwards force on the opponent as possible, but you should always allow the uprightness or otherwise of your opponent's posture to determine just how much of this upwards force you should attempt to use.

In the case of an opponent who is about your own height and who takes up a defensive bent forward position, you will very often have to move away from your normal method of executing your speciality even further, so much so that at the latter end of the technique, in the case of tsuri-komi-goshi, you have to turn it into a tai-otoshi-makikomi technique.

And if you do tsuri-komi-goshi against a short person who adopts a bent or crouched defensive posture, you have to pull him up with your right hand, and should always be prepared, if you find it difficult to throw him just with the use of your right buttock, to at the latter end of the move raise your right leg and go into a harai-makikomi technique.

These few examples will help you to understand what is meant by adapting your usual method of executing your speciality to your opponent's posture. Of course the way you adapt your technique will depend on what your speciality in throwing technique is and on what constitutes a problematical posture on the part of your opponent in the case of your own particular speciality. But with regular practising of your speciality, you should have no difficulty in recognizing these problematical postures and developing effective methods of adapting your usual method of throwing to them.

What is also necessary to the judo player if he wants to be able effectively to handle awkward opponents, is to take particular notice of the different ways opponents can position themselves, after he attacks them with his speciality, with the object of preventing him from throwing them. Very often opponents will react in such a way to your throwing attempt, that they finish up in positions which do not lend themselves at all to your having any chance of throwing them by simply making what could be called an adaptation of your original throw. This is usually the case when in order to prevent you from throwing them they force their body as far as possible in the direction completely opposite to that in which you are trying to throw them. For example, if you use a forward throwing technique against them, they will often attempt to pull the right side of their jacket out of your left hand grip by dragging the upper part of their body right back and pushing their hips and thighs strongly forward. Or, if you attempt a rear throwing technique, they will push the upper part of their body strongly forward and tense their legs forcefully backward.

When your opponent reacts in this extremely defensive fashion, it is almost impossible to force your first technique through to a successful conclusion. By reacting in this manner, however, your opponent is not in a position to offer much resistance to techniques applied in the opposite direction to that of your first technique. You must, therefore, decide by practice which technique will enable you to take advantage of this momentary weakness in your opponent's posture. What technique you decide to practise so as to prepare yourself for these occasions when they crop up in contest will of course be determined by which throwing technique you specialize in. This is so because the technique you choose will have to be one which enables you to move from your favourite throwing technique position in the most efficient manner possible, so as to position yourself with the speed necessary to take advantage of your opponent's temporary weakness and throw him with the second technique.

The following classical methods of moving from one technique into another will illustrate quite clearly what is meant by the foregoing. When your opponent resists an uchi-mata, a hane-goshi, or a tsuri-komi-goshi throw, immediately throw him to his rear with o-uchi-gari. When he resists morote-seoi-nage, throw him to his rear with ko-uchi-gari. When he resists o-soto-gari, follow it up with ashi-guruma if your right leg is not far behind his right leg. When he resists o-uchi-gari, you can often throw him with uchi-mata to his front if you make a very rapid turn with your body as soon as you feel his resistance to your o-uchi-gari.

Finally, however, it must be stated that unless you develop your favourite throwing technique into a really powerful movement, your opponent will have no need to resist it sufficiently to enable you to move into a natural continuation technique and throw him with it. It can be seen, therefore, that any real success that you achieve in judo depends on how much work and thought you put into developing your main throwing technique.

48 FORTY-EIGHTH PRINCIPLE

Don't put the cart before the horse by trying to teach judo before you have done quite a lot of judo yourself. Wait until you have been graded to at least First or Second Dan before attempting to influence others as a teacher.

In order to get to know enough about this very complex and difficult activity called judo so that you can be in a position to teach it to others, there is only one thing to do. And that is to get down to the business of practising judo frequently and regularly for a fairly long period of time. The longer the better if you aspire to becoming a worthwhile teacher.

Reading books on judo, taking lessons in judo, thinking about judo, are all very well and can be of great value to you, if you use them as a means to improve your judo ability on the judo practice mats or in the contest area, and not to improve your ability in the conversation area in the saloon bar when spouting forth on judo to those whose real knowledge of the art is even less than your own.

In order, therefore, to make best use of these three valuable aids to the development of true judo ability, get into the habit of putting into practice the advice, hints, instruction, etc., which your reading and your teachers give you, and also the theories which you can evolve from thinking about judo. This habit will not only be of great value to your own personal development as a person with great confidence in your own ability on the judo mat, but it will also gradually enable you to build up a large store house of very useful information which, when you eventually turn your attention to teaching, can be in turn passed on to your pupils.

You will, in fact, if you give yourself the chance to develop as a judo player along these lines, gradually become a walking encyclopaedia of irrefutable judo truths and facts, and you will also develop that which is essential to a teacher of judo, an almost uncanny sense for distinguishing between that which is possible and that which is impossible.

Frequent and regular judo training, in other words, acts like a purifying mechanism which gradually eliminates from your mind all those ideas and conceptions of judo which are worthless and time-wasting, and retains only those which are of real value.

Attaining to this stage of purification, as it were, requires time and effort, but the personal rewards of true ability and true knowledge are in themselves well worth the time and effort spent. You can also at this stage go on, confident in your credentials, as it were, to start teaching others, who because you have done such a good job with your first pupil, yourself, will benefit enormously from your instruction and influence. And as your experience as a teacher increases, you will find that more and more you will, for the increased benefit of your pupils, be able to put to better and better use the knowledge and experience which your own practical judo training has given you and will continue to give you. For simply because you start to teach should not mean that you should give up practising yourself. In fact the best teachers are those who can combine the practice of judo with the teaching of it. Of course, there are many excellent teachers who because of age cannot possibly undertake this dual role. But with their practical and teaching experience it is no longer necessary for them to attempt to.

If, however, you have never taken the trouble to get a good grounding in judo yourself by a fairly long experience in the practice of judo, and start to teach it to others, you will misdirect and misinform these unfortunates so much that they will in most cases give up this wonderful activity in despair. And it is mainly for this tragic reason that the teaching of judo should only be in the hands of those whose own personal practical experience equips them for it.

49 FORTY-NINTH PRINCIPLE

Due to his inability to pass on his knowledge via the spoken English word easily, by far the best way to get the most out of a Japanese instructor is to practise with him regularly, and also to observe his every little movement while he is practising with others, then attempt to copy him.

To teach in one's own native language is a difficult enough thing to do if one really wishes to do a first class job of teaching. But to do a first class job of teaching having to speak in a language other than one's native language is almost an impossibility, unless one becomes very fluent and skilled in the use of the foreign language. And even then it is still difficult, and one never comes to be able to use a foreign language with the same facility and great naturalness that characterizes the speech of a native speaker. And without this natural facility with a language, it is almost the work of a genius to be able to explain in detail the very many subtle points of a subject which have to be explained when teaching. And as the genius is of course a very rare type of individual indeed, there are very few people who can teach a subject satisfactorily in a language other than their own native tongue.

Of course, we have all heard of the person who claims to be able to speak, and understand too mark you, several languages like the respective native speakers of these languages. I can tell you now, quite categorically, that this is a lot of bunkum. There are, of course, those people who are to a certain extent capable both of speaking and understanding several foreign languages, but they will, if they are honest and mature, agree with me when I say it is impossible to master these languages so that they will ever come anywhere near to handling these languages like a native speaker does. In fact to do this with even one foreign language is a remarkable feat in itself. A feat moreover which literally requires a lifetime's study and practice. The real polyglot, therefore, is quite non-existent.

All this slowly dawned on me during my seven years stay in Japan, during which time I put a great deal of effort into learning the Japanese language. I was until that time I suppose just as gullible as anyone else who had never attempted to learn a foreign language when it came to believing the fallacies surrounding this activity.

But it was not until I had been in Japan for some four or five years that I had the opportunity to put myself in the same position as the many Japanese judo teachers in England, Canada, and Japan from whom I had received instructions in judo in English, and discover just what a difficult job it must have been for them to have to teach in a foreign tongue.

Because it was at this time that I began to teach English to Japanese who had almost no real knowledge of the language at all, and I had therefore to conduct the lessons in Japanese. Hitherto, I had taught English only to those Japanese whose knowledge of English was good enough to enable me to use nothing but English throughout the whole of the lesson. Anyway, I had been in Japan for a long time, with a knowledge and fluency in Japanese which can only be gained by living in the country for this length of time and using the language every day, and I therefore assumed that I was sufficiently equipped for the job of teaching English to Japanese who had no knowledge of English worthy of mention and conducting the lessons in their own language.

I soon realized that there was a large difference between holding an ordinary conversation in a foreign language and having to use the same medium for the purpose of teaching. The latter is much more difficult, if one is to do a good job of teaching. The problem is one not only of having to present in the foreign language the material for a lesson in an orderly, comprehensible, and intelligent fashion, but also to have to use one's power of comprehension to the full so that one can understand the often long and complicated questions which are put to one, and then have to give satisfactory replies and explanations to these questions. All of course in a foreign language.

Well, as I have said, I had been in Japan about five years at the time I started conducting English classes in Japanese – which may seem rather odd in a way, but it's the only way you can do it if you are teaching Japanese with very little knowledge of English. And I must say, in spite of the fact that I had been in the country studying Japanese for this length of time, I found that using Japanese as a medium for teaching was very difficult indeed. And although with time the difficulty diminished somewhat, it was always a strain.

Imagine, therefore, just how much more difficult it must be for a Japanese judo teacher, to teach his subject in your own language, when you consider that due to the fact that he will usually remain teaching in your country for only a year or two his opportunities for learning your language are not very great.

And it is on the foregoing lines of reasoning that this forty-ninth principle is based.

50 FIFTIETH PRINCIPLE

If you decide to build up a technique on the side which is not natural to you (to build up a left-handed technique if you normally do right-handed techniques, or to build up a right-handed technique if you normally do left-handed techniques), make sure that you give a lot of thought to your choice of technique, and also seek the advice of a high-grade judo man. If these things are not done, you can easily spend a lot of time and effort on a technique the opportunities for executing which are extremely limited.

We shall assume in this article that you are a right-hander. If you are a left hander, simply adapt what is said to this fact.

It is almost impossible, for the vast majority of judo players anyway, to build up a technique on the side which is not natural to him to the point where it is as powerful as techniques which he does on his natural side. Unless, of course, for the purposes of strategy he decides to specialize in left-handed judo even though he is a natural right hander. But we are not referring to this, we are simply referring to the person who is a natural right hander and who specializes in right-handed technique and who decides to add to his repertoire of right-handed technique a left handed throw.

Because of the comparative weakness of a left-handed throw, therefore, the left-handed technique which we choose must be one which will enable us to take advantage of frequently recurring good opportunities and enable us to use it naturally and effectively after creating by feints those opportunities for throwing on the left which our right-handed techniques are capable of creating.

The good opportunity which crops up mostly is the one created by a left-handed opponent who takes up a rather extreme left-handed stance. This is a position which you can use to good advantage with left ippon-seoi-nage (one handed shoulder throw). Of course it is not very effective if your opponent is much shorter than yourself. Another technique which you can use to good advantage against the same position is left kata-gurume (shoulder wheel). Again, however, the assumption is that your opponent is not much shorter than yourself, if the technique is to be effective.

The reason why these two techniques are popular as left-hand techniques with right-handers is, however, not only because they can be used with effect against left-handers, but also because in order to use them it is not necessary to take a grip of the right side of your opponent's jacket. This enables you to make it difficult for your opponent (assuming he relies on a two-handed grip that is) to throw you by simply refusing to allow him to take a grip with his right hand while you wait for an opportunity to use these techniques. Mr. Okano, the world judo champion, uses left ippon-seoi-nage with tremendous effect, even though he is a natural right-hander. And Mr. Inokuma, another previous world champion, who although a right-hander has a very good left kata-guruma.

If at first you take a normal grip on your opponent's jacket with both hands, you can also use the ippon-seoi-nage or kata-guruma on the left to take advantage of opportunities for throwing on the left which you create by feints with your right-hand technique.

In fact, all techniques on the left can be used for this purpose. But the fact of the matter is that certain techniques on the left used by right-handers have come to be considered much more practicable for this purpose than others. And by far the most popular left-handed technique used by right-handers in Japan is left o-guruma. This is a favourite of Kisaburo Watanabe, famous Japanese stylist and ex Asian Games Champion, whose judo had such an impact on British judo men during his stay here in London as judo instructor at the Rensbuden and Budokwai clubs. Left o-guruma is also a favourite technique of the ex Japanese judo champion Mr. Sakeguchi. Among British judo-ka the most famous exponents of left o-guruma are Mr. T. P. Leggett, Mr. D. Bloss, and Mr. Warwick P. Stepto, all Japan-trained high grade judo men of the Budokwai club. Of course, o-guruma experts will often alternate between this technique and ashi-guruma, as both techniques have a great deal in common. And although these techniques are more suitable for the tall judo player, players of other heights can easily adapt themselves to them. I remember seeing Mr. Iwata, a truly amazing judo expert, although very short, hurling a man much taller than himself through the air with o-guruma in the All Japan Championships.

Left ippon-seoi-nage, which we have already dealt with, is next in line in popularity with those who are not too tall for it.

Another technique on the left which gets a fairly good following, again among players who are not too tall, is sode-tsurikomi-goshi. And it is this technique which recalls for me the very happy two years which I spent at the Vancouver judo club in Canada and the fine judo men such as Tom Tamoto, John Iwamoto, Cliff Aiken, Ben Cook, Malcolm Jones, Fred Matt, Mike Djeldahl, Chris Kato from Seattle, and many others, whom I had the pleasure of knowing and practising with. As it was here that I saw Bobby Nakashima, another prominent member of the club, execute left sode-tsurikomi-goshi with more expertise than I had ever seen it done before. I remember seeing him use it to defeat Fred Matt in a major Canadian tournament. And this was no mean feat as Matt is undoubtedly one of the strongest non-Japanese judo players I personally have ever gone against in contest. It was he who gave Mr. Sone the Japanese judo champion such a hard time in the world judo championships of 1960 in Paris. Another good sode-tsurikomi-goshi man on the left is that great Australian judo player Ron Ford, whom I became good friends with when we trained together in Japan. I do not think that I have ever met a person who displayed as much enthusiasm for judo training as Ford did. The most powerful of the Japanese sode-tsuri-komi-goshi men I practised with in Japan was Mr. Ito of Nichi Daigaku (university of Japan), who used to combine it with right ko-uchi-gari and right o-uchi-gari.

The next in line in popularity as a left-handed technique for right-handers is left uchi-mata. I well remember Mr. Chikashi Nakanishi, an old friend of mine, surprising everybody at the Budokwai with this technique when he trained and taught there at the same time as Mr. Kawamura, 7th Dan Kodokan, and Mr. Ono another great judo man from Waseda university. He was a natural right hander but he had built up an uchi mata on the left which was very strong indeed. Perhaps he had been influenced in his choice by that Great judo player and teacher Mr. Osawa from the same university as Mr. Nakanishi, Waseda, as Mr. Osawa had a beautiful left handed repertoire. Another person who impressed me greatly with his combination of right o-soto-gari and right tai-otoshi and left uchi-mata was Mr. Yamagishi, who threw quite a large number of opponents with his very aggressive left uchi-mata. And although uchi-mata is generally regarded as a tall man's technique, when it is done on the left against a person reacting strongly to his front to some right-hand technique, it can be pulled off by people who are not tall.

Left o-soto-gari is also a technique which can be used as a left technique by a right-hander, but one has to make sure that the circumstances are ideal before attempting it as it is very easy to be countered by your opponent when trying this throw.

The foregoing techniques are the left-hand techniques which are used most by people who are otherwise right-handed. But as said before, any technique on the left can be combined, if practised regularly, with your right-hand repertoire of technique. But to be on the safe side surely it is better to build up one of these foregoing throws, the effectiveness of which has been proved by top class judo men, instead of risking wasting your time by choosing another. In fact, although left hane-goshi or left morote-seoi-nage can be done by a strong right hander against a weak opponent, it is extremely difficult for him to throw a strong opponent with these two techniques. And that is why these two techniques are hardly ever used by right-handers as left techniques.

The reason for this will become clear if you study the mechanics of the technique of the left-handed throws which are popular and the ones which are not. In the case of the former, it is not that difficult to adapt one's hold on the opponent's jacket and one's normal foot work to what is necessary in this respect when doing one of these left techniques. In the case of the unpopular left techniques, however, you will find that this adaptation is almost completely out of the question when you are up against an experienced opponent. I learnt this fact from practising regularly at The Budokwai with my first Kodokan teacher, that great Judo-ka Mr. Teizo Kawamura, 7th Dan.

THE END

Printed in Great Britain
by Amazon

19089246R00078